THE PARABLE OF THE PEACOCK

A Read-Aloud Picture Book for 2020 Voters

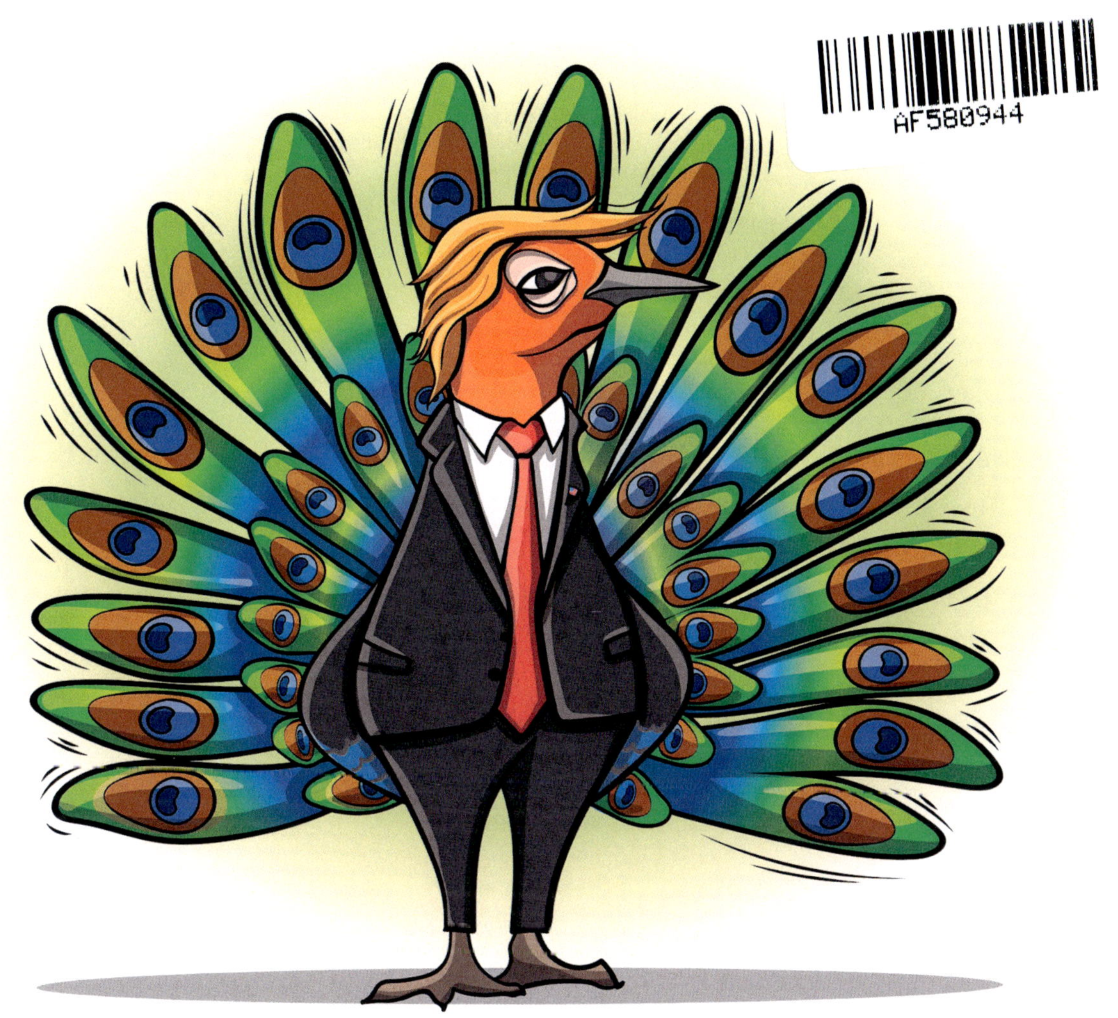

Written by Brent Bohlen

Illustrated by Oksana Basarab

Salvage America Publications

Salvage America Publications
ISBN: 978-1-7335757-9-9

10 9 8 7 6 5 4 3 2 1

The Parable of the Peacock

DEDICATION

This book is dedicated to our nation's founders, who gave citizens the right to speak freely and poke fun at their leaders, and to journalists, who work tirelessly and occasionally at significant risk to speak truth to power.

ACKNOWLEDGMENTS

You would not be holding this book in your hand if it were not for the Herculean effort of Jeff Salvage, a man of innumerable talents and a dear friend for the decade since he published my first book. When I initially mentioned the project to him I had a manuscript and no illustrations. His enthusiasm, stamina and bottomless well of knowledge made this book a reality. His suggestions made this book better, but he never pushed too far – all decisions on the contents and the responsibility for them are mine alone.

You would not enjoy this book nearly as much without the marvelous artwork of Oksana Basarab. Some people find a spouse on the Internet. I found an artist of wonderful talent who can transform simply sketched suggestions into captivating illustrations. The marriage of my words and her art could not have been a more perfect union.

I would not have enjoyed the long life I have experienced nearly as much if I hadn't had my wife, Mary, by my side. For nearly 50 years now she has been there to support and love me, and I hope we have many more years together.

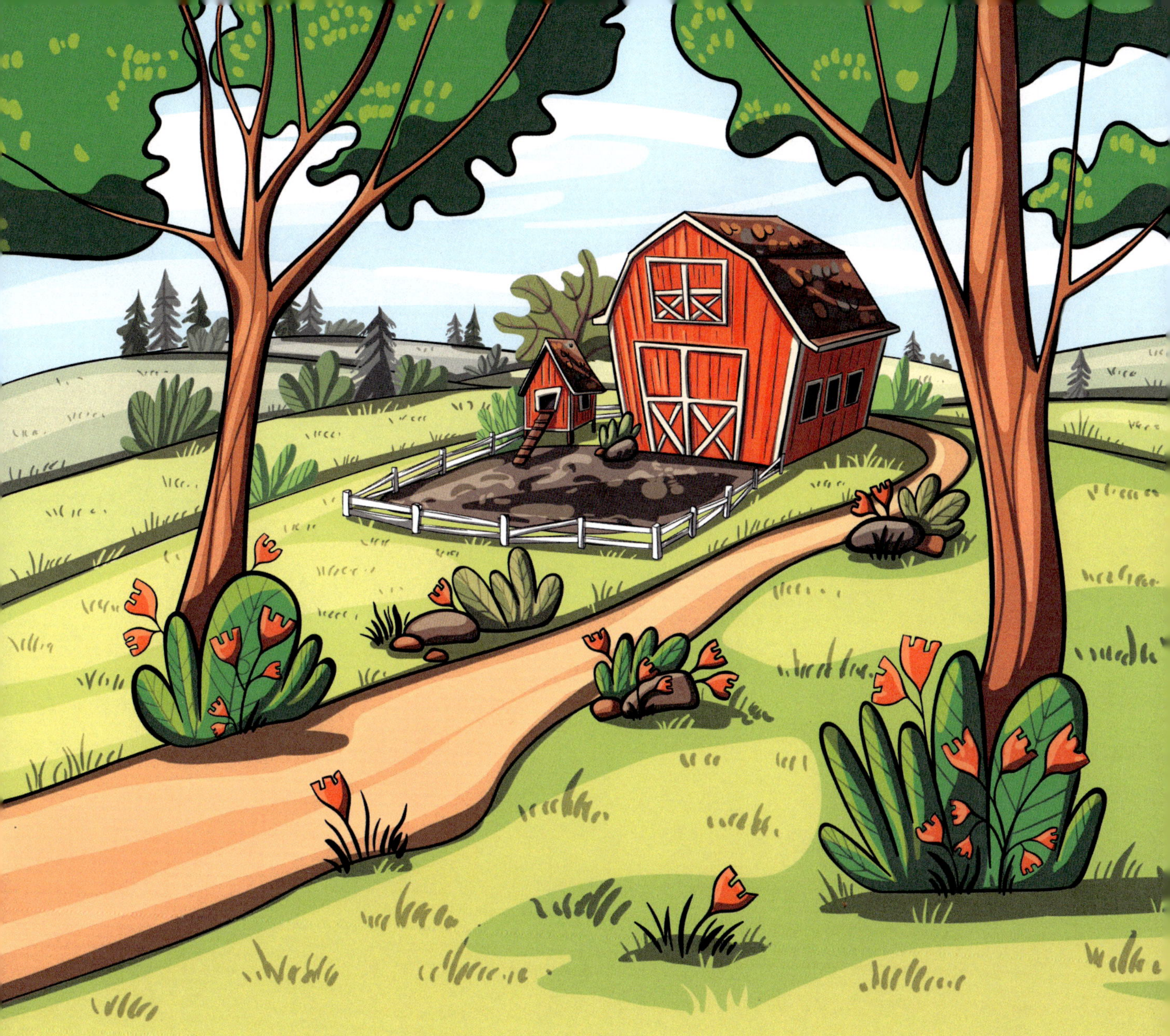

Once upon a time, not so long ago
And not far, as far-away places go,
There was a barnyard land, vibrant and large
Led by one elected to be in charge.
Years on end the animals were content
As they were well-served by their government.

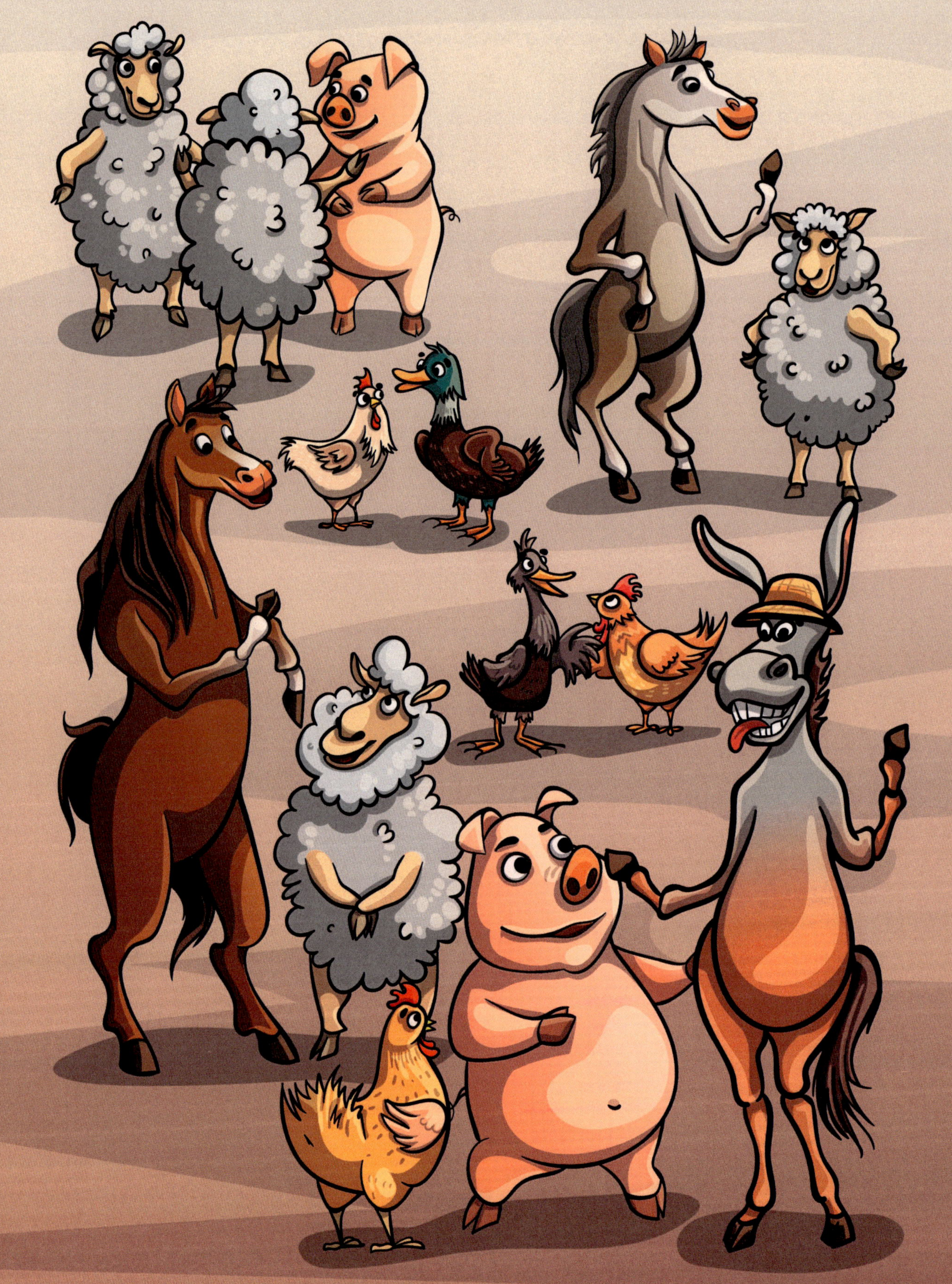

Most leaders were either a pig or a horse,
And some horses were jackasses, of course.
On further thought, and giving them their due,
Many of the pigs were jackasses, too.
There were chickens and ducks within the keep,
But mostly there were lots and lots of sheep.

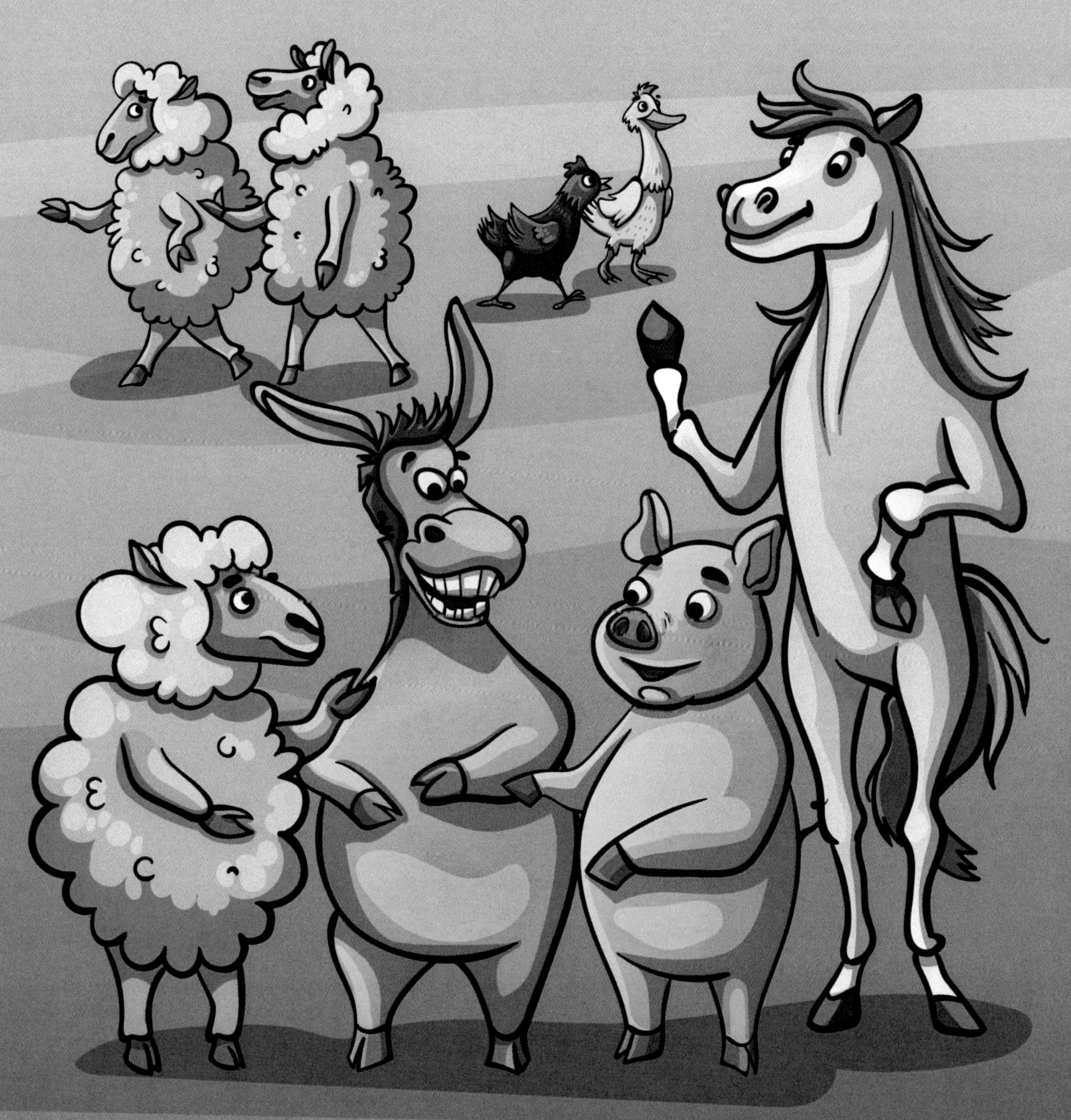

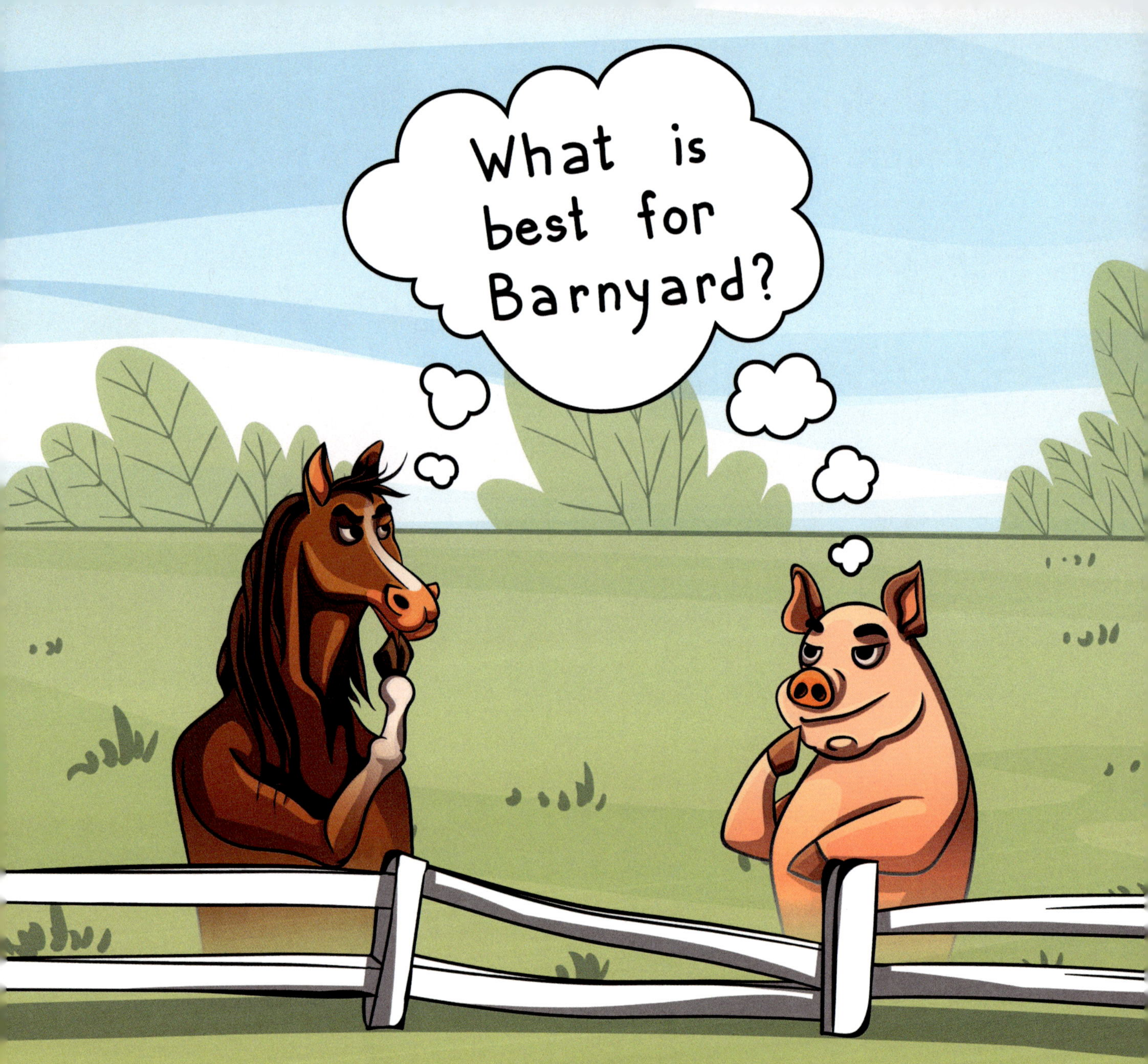

Generally, whether a horse or a pig,
Each of the leaders saw the picture big.
Though oft' tempted, they tried to do their part
To keep everyone's best interests at heart.
If voters felt things were going off course,
They'd switch from horse to pig, or pig to horse.

Things slowly changed over a length of time,
And the barnyard no longer seemed sublime.
The horses and pigs from whence leaders came
Were more concerned whether the leader's name
Was that of a horse or a pig, you see,
Than whether the leader served you and me.

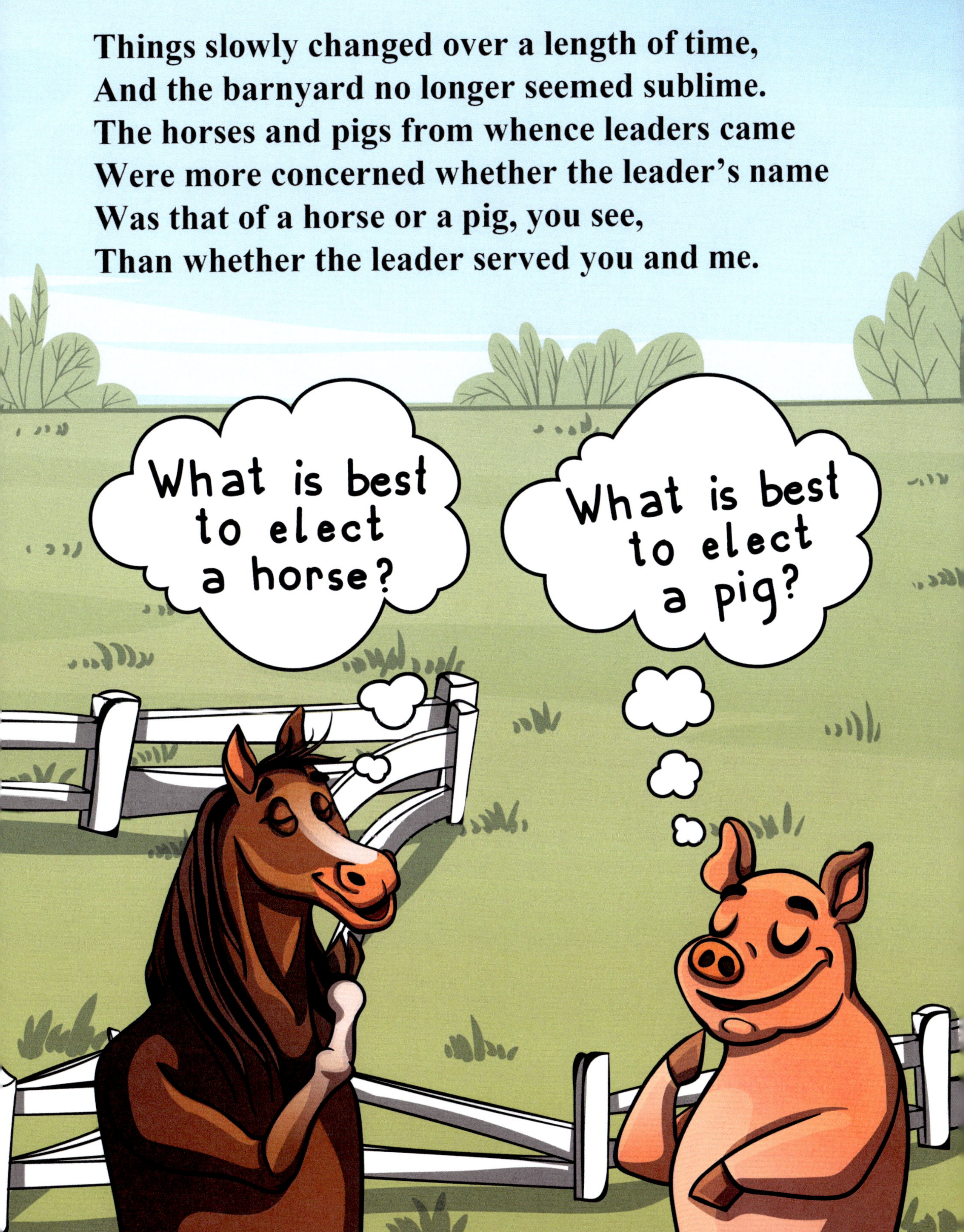

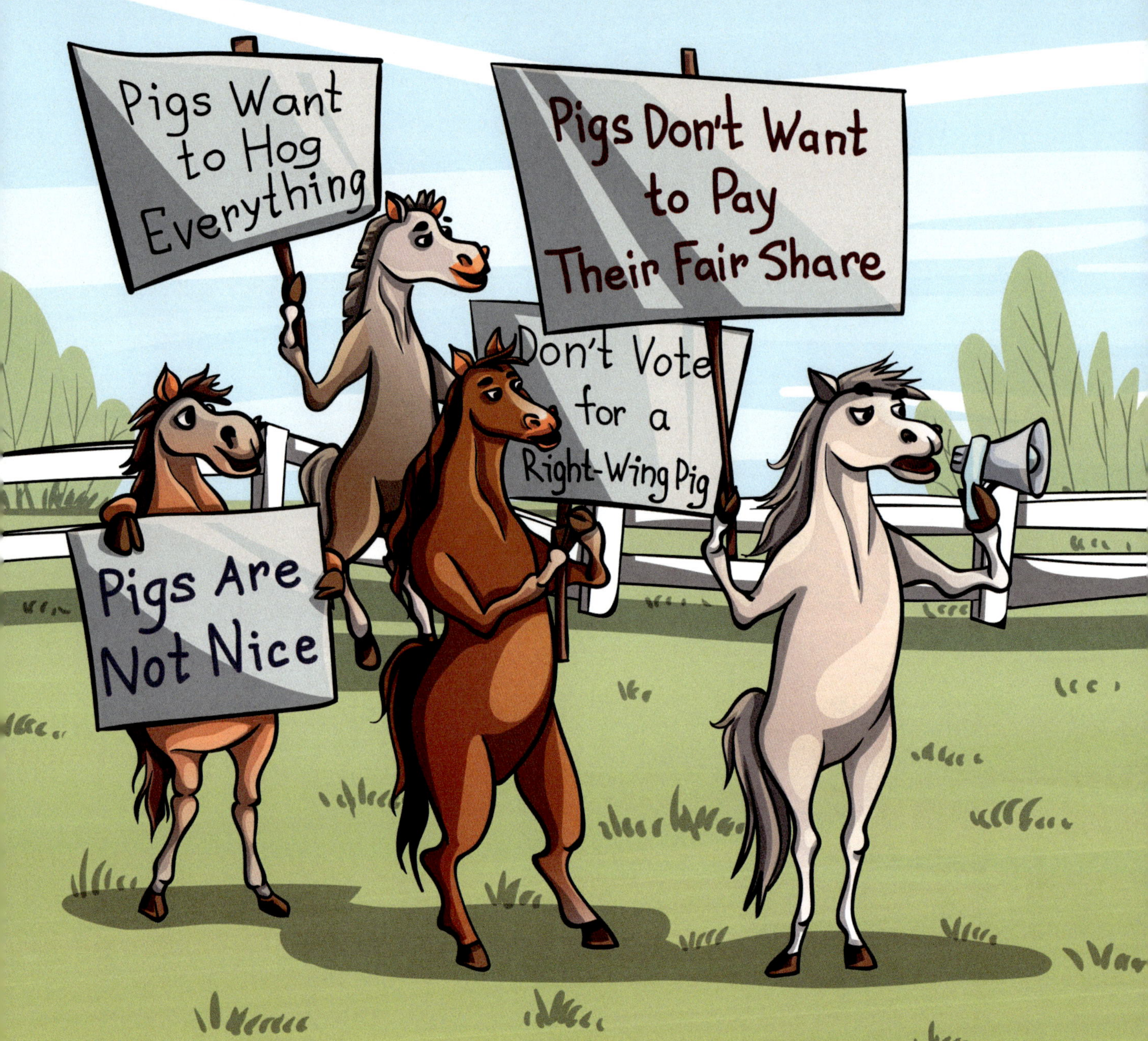

Their basic beliefs differed from the start,
But each new year they grew further apart.
It's no wonder the barnyard got the blues –
The following statements captured their views:
"Pigs defend selfishness with laissez-faire!"
And "Socialist horses think lazy's fair!"

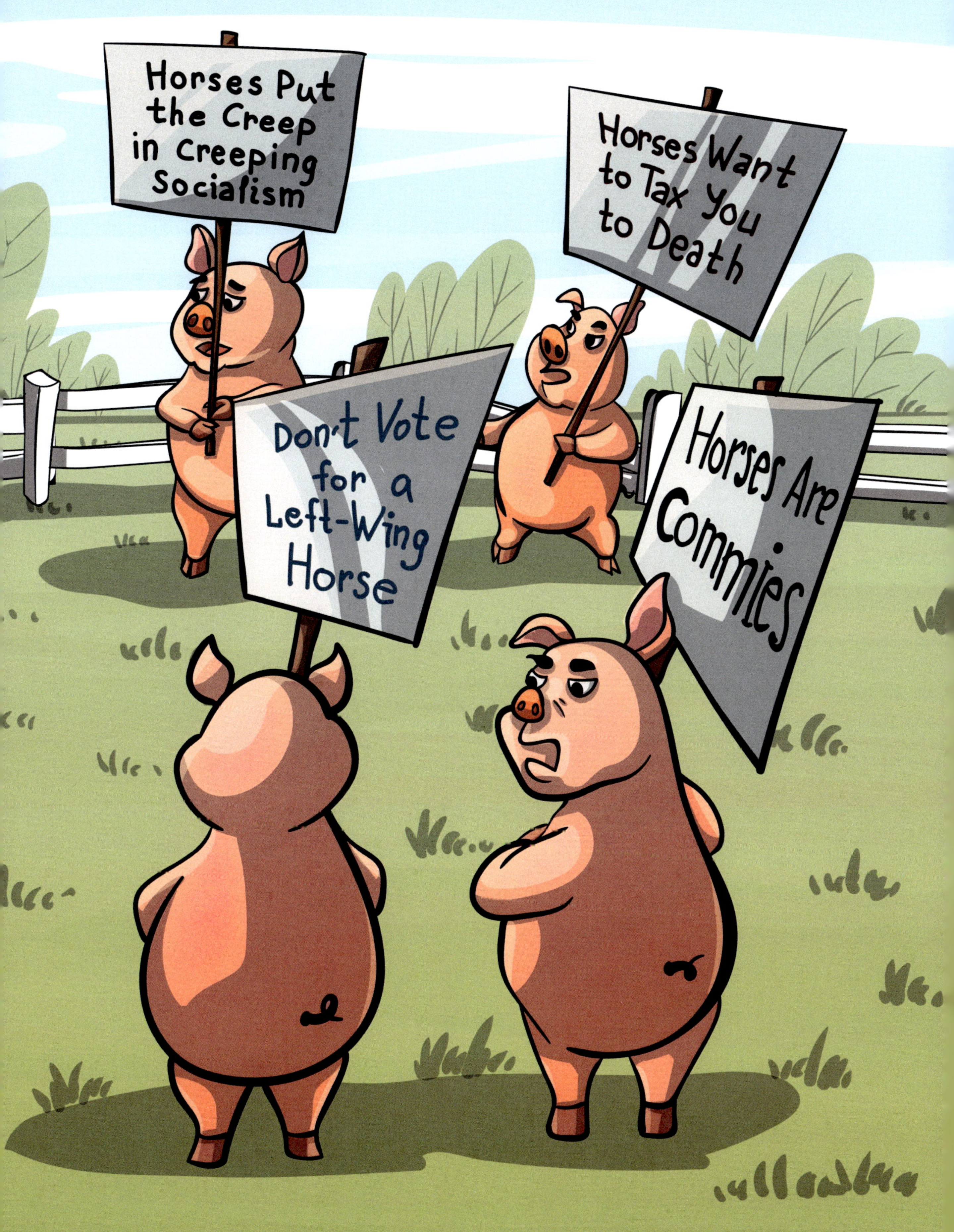
Horses Put the Creep in Creeping Socialism
Horses Want to Tax You to Death
Don't Vote for a Left-Wing Horse
Horses Are Commies

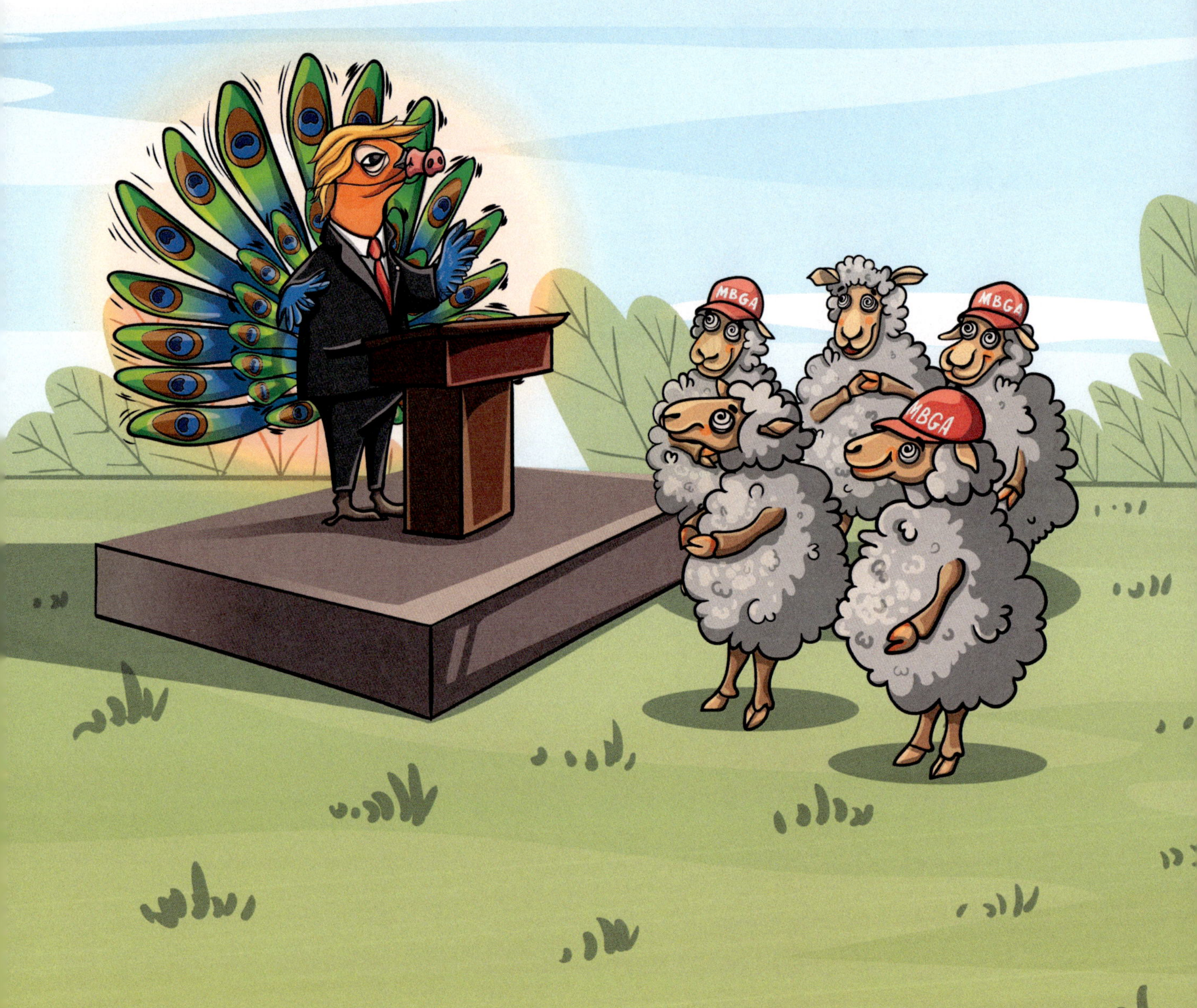

A prideful peacock claimed he was a pig
And said he'd be leader with plans SO big.
He promised to Make Barnyard Great Again
Because he was the greatest there had ever been.
But he mostly preened, spread his showy tail –
'Twas enough, though, to cause sheep brains to fail.

The manual for all diagnoses
Of mental issues up to psychoses
Includes Peacock's portrait at center stage
At the top of the narcissism page.
Even Peacock will heartily agree,
"On any subject – It's all about ME!"

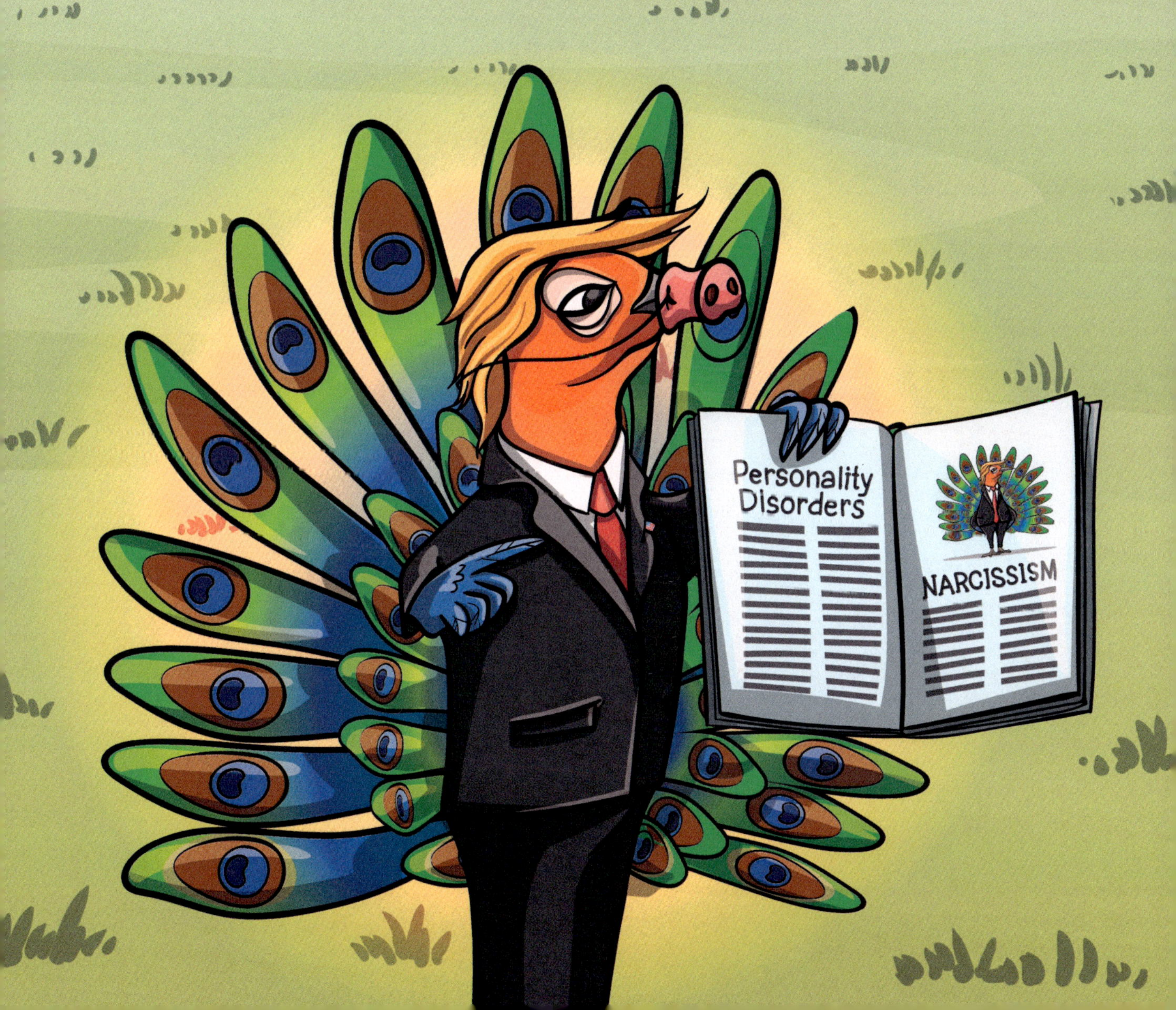

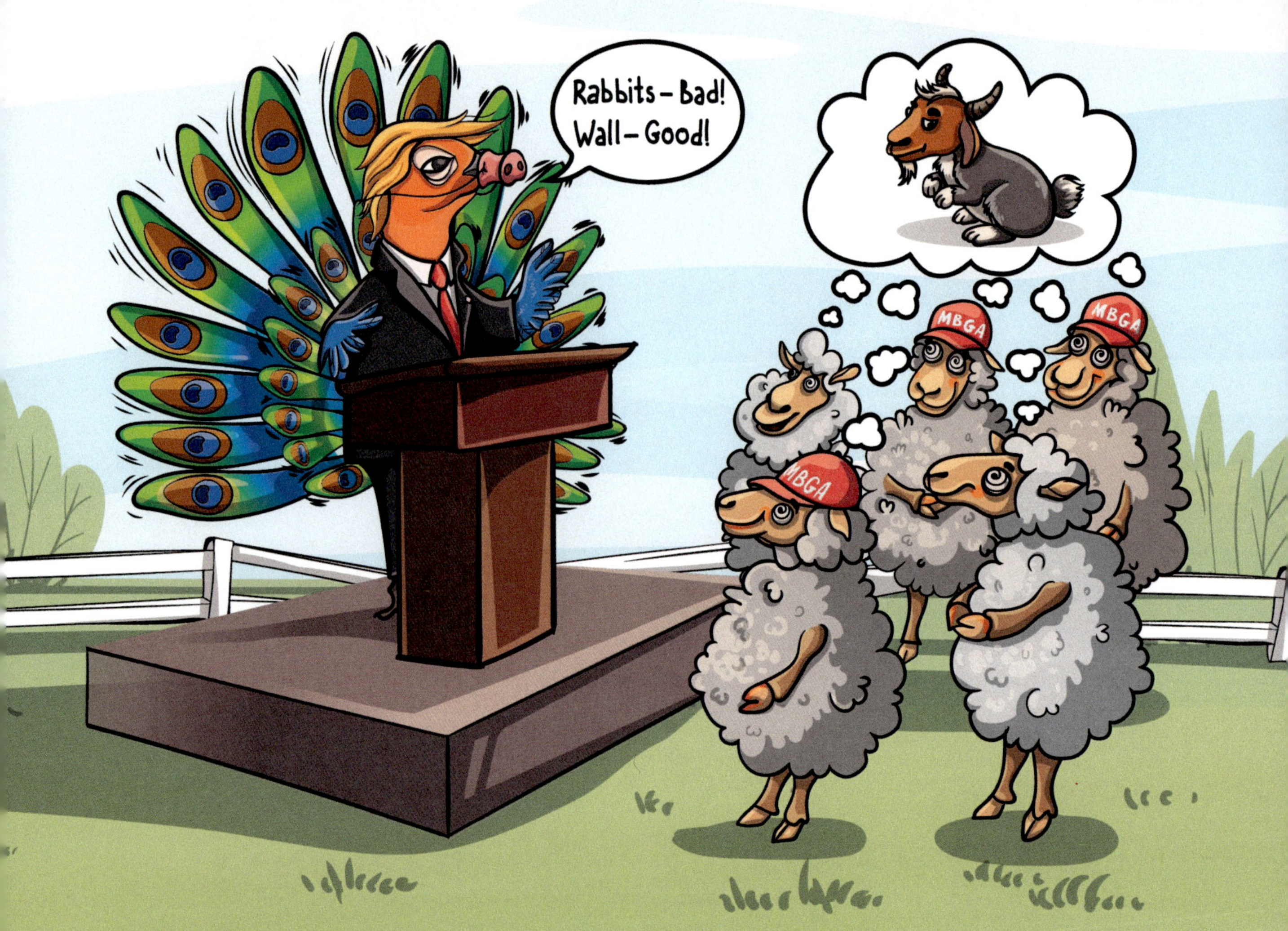

For years pigs had promoted tribalism
By misappropriating Bible-ism.
But the pesky peacock added a twist
That the barnyard's poor sheep could not resist.
Their problems were caused by rabbits, he said,
Coming from other lands, something to dread.
He promised that all their problems would fall
If they'd let him build a beautiful wall.
The wily peacock, a wizard of note,
Turned each poor bunny into a scapegoat.

Following the fowl was normal for sheep.
But what really caused a loss of sleep
Was when the peacock's strong spell of magic
Led to surprising events so tragic.
Almost all of the PIGS turned into SHEEP!
Even some HORSES made the leap!
It was more than just unbelievable;
It was effing, damn inconceivable!

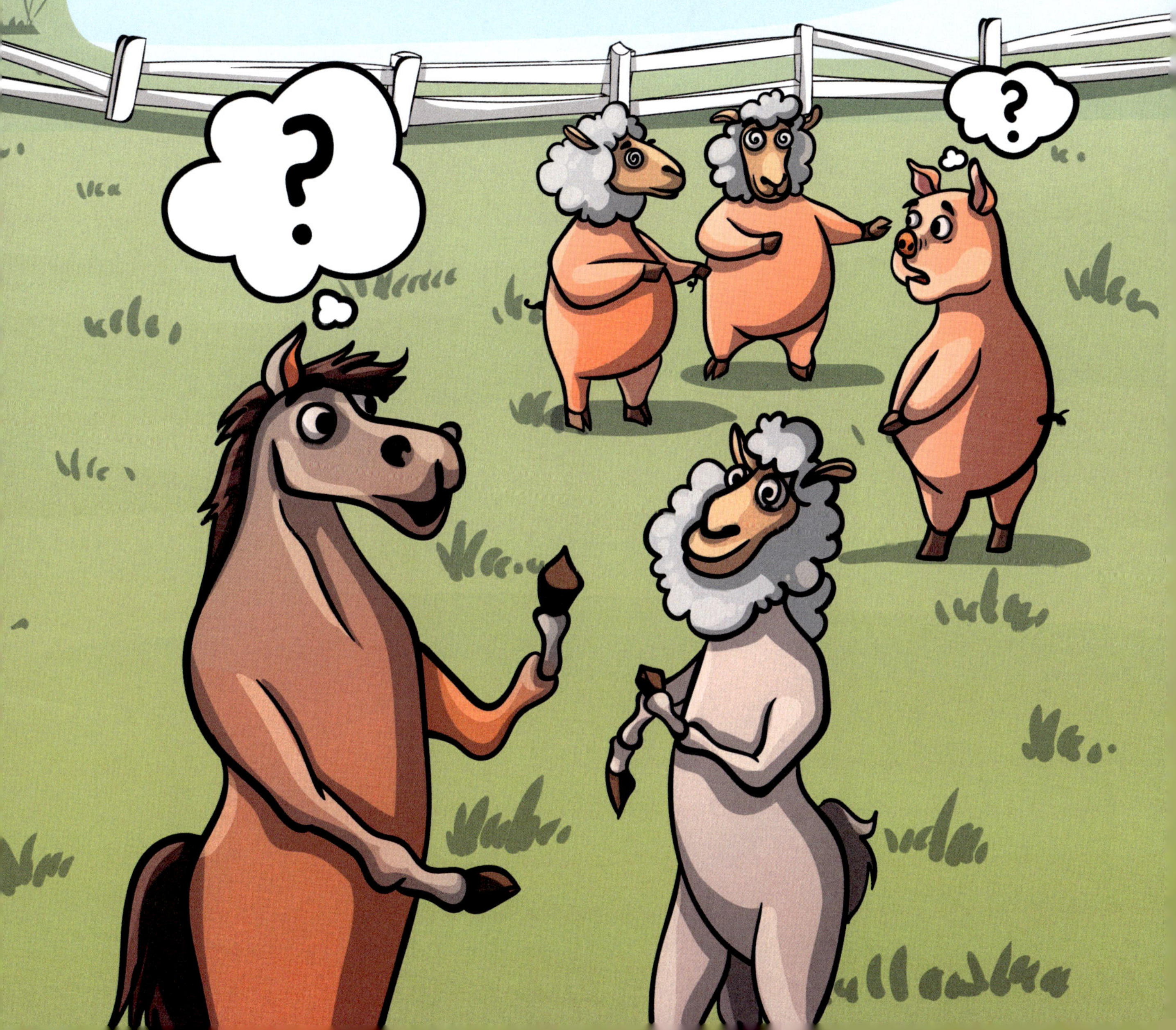

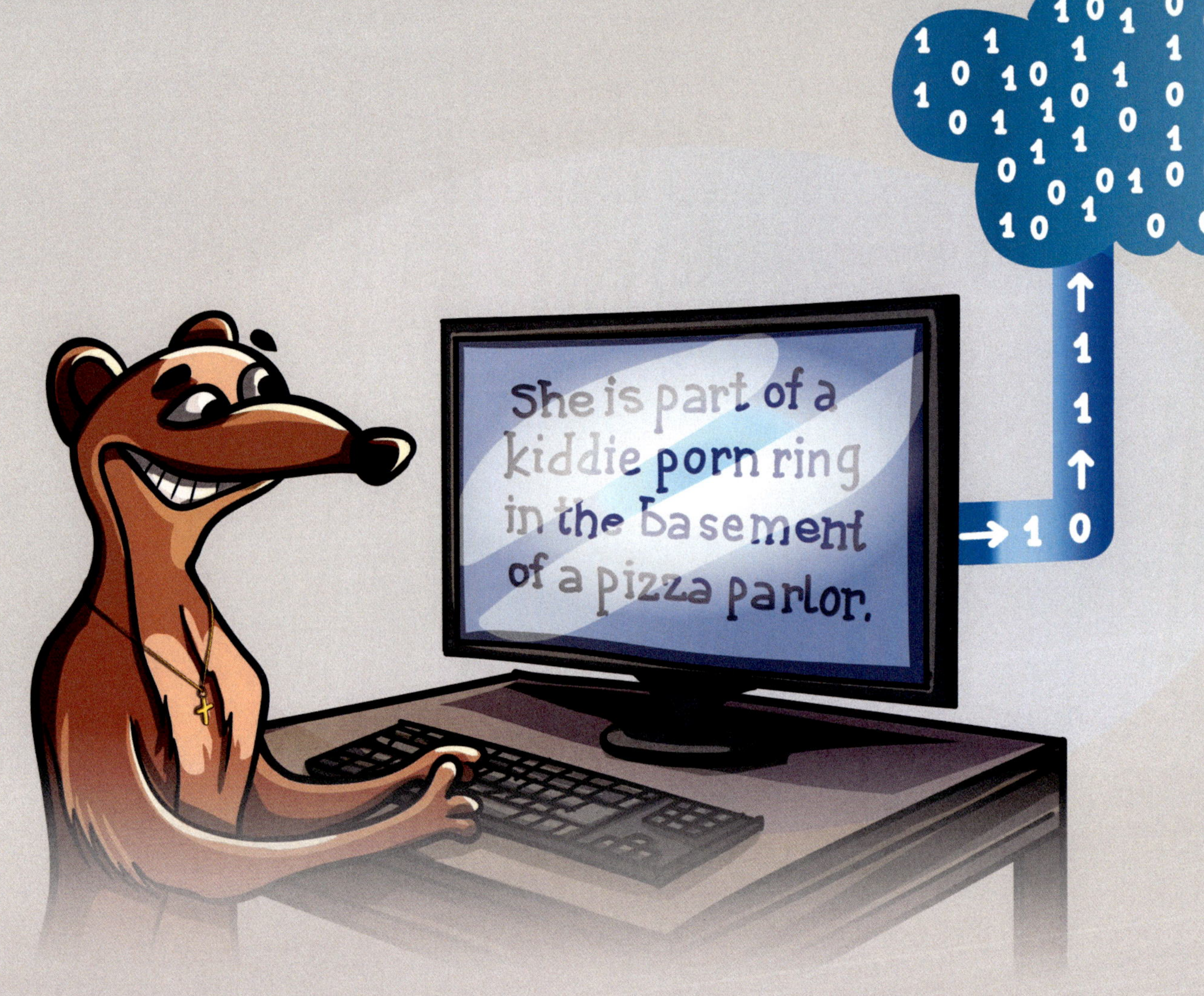

As the day to choose a leader drew nigh
The shameless peacock piled lie upon lie.
And no one knew he got a helping hand
From a mean weasel in a far-off land.
The weasel lied, too. It was so crappy.
He helped by making the sheep unhappy.
Weasel did his deeds by hook and by crook,
Using fake news on Twitter and Facebook.

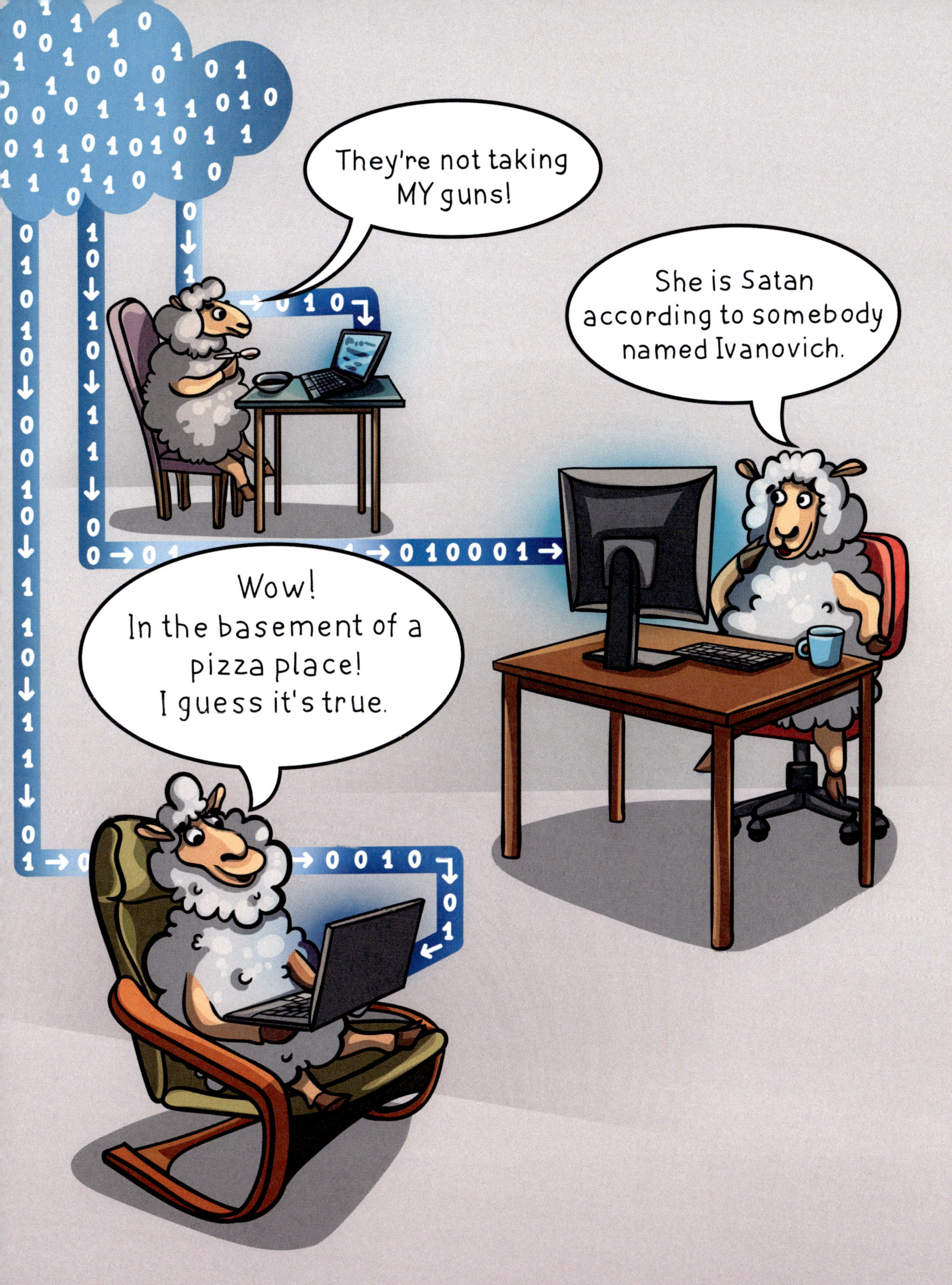

They're not taking MY guns!
She is Satan according to somebody named Ivanovich.
Wow! In the basement of a pizza place! I guess it's true.

Election day produced an upset BIG!
They picked the BIRD who claimed to be a PIG!
After taking the oath, he whined out loud
As he lied and lied and resized the crowd.
Peacock planned some parties to strut his stuff.
He sought out donations – more than enough.
The parties were fine, not over the top.
Couldn’t spend it all. Where did those bucks stop?

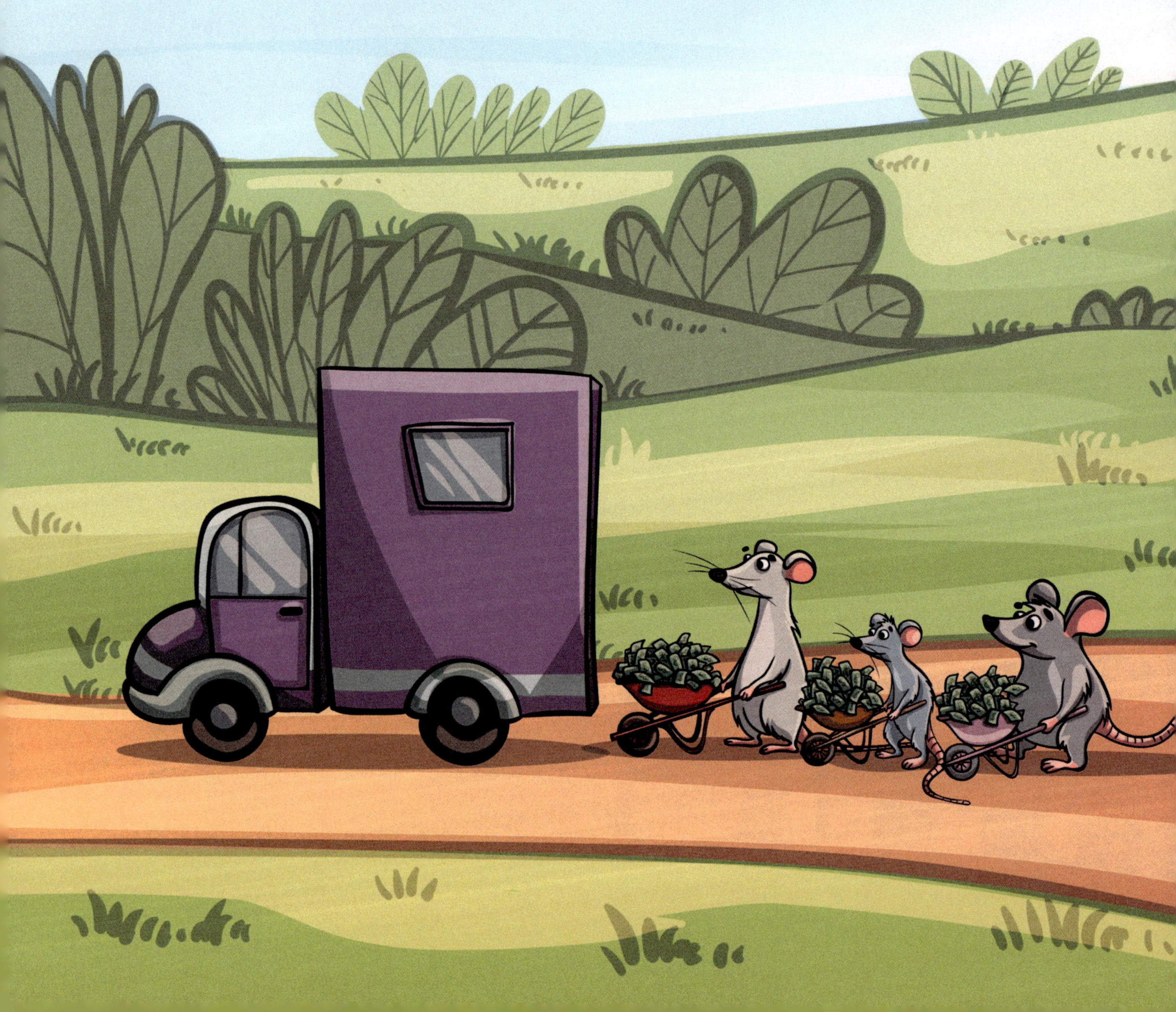

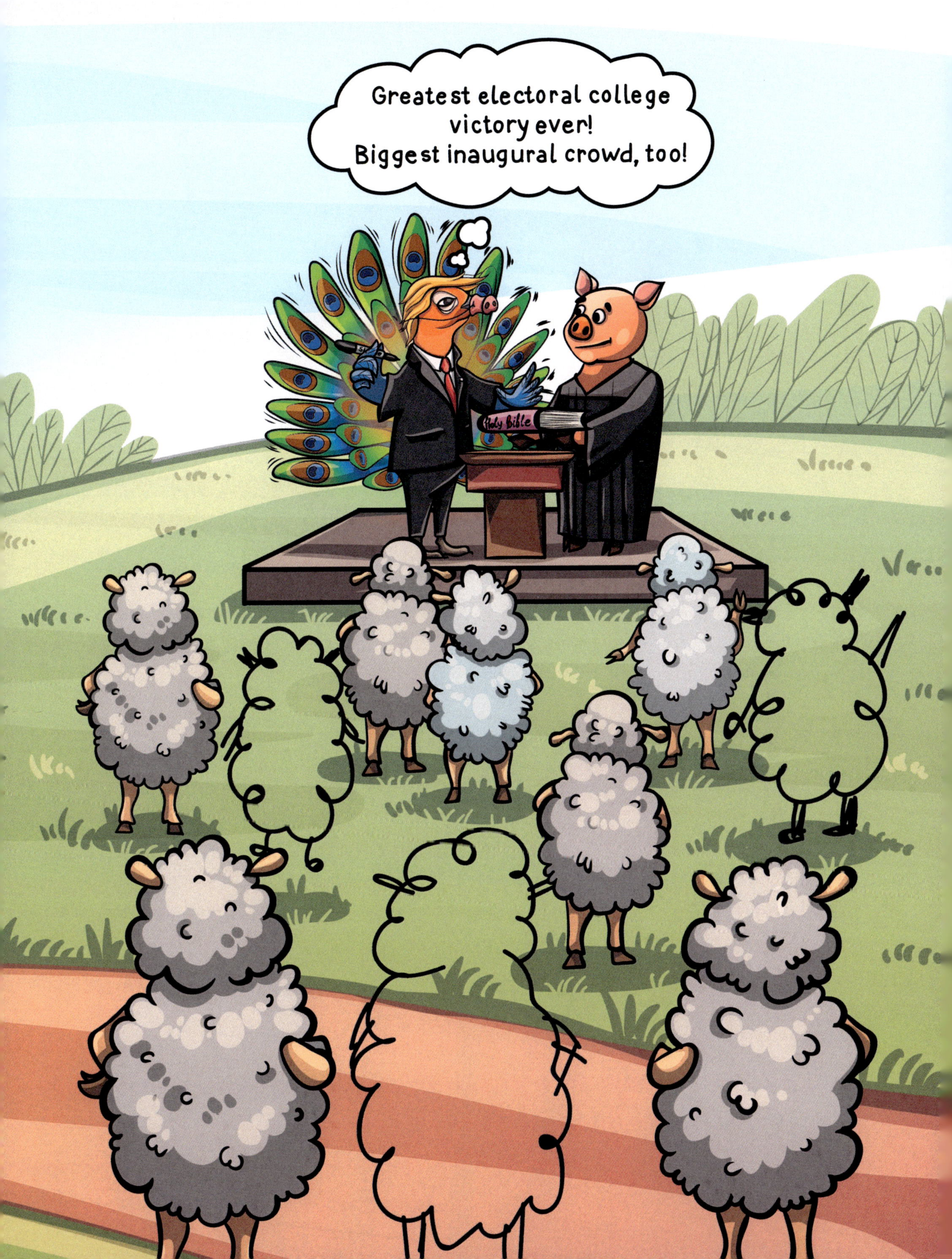
Greatest electoral college
victory ever!
Biggest inaugural crowd, too!
Holy Bible

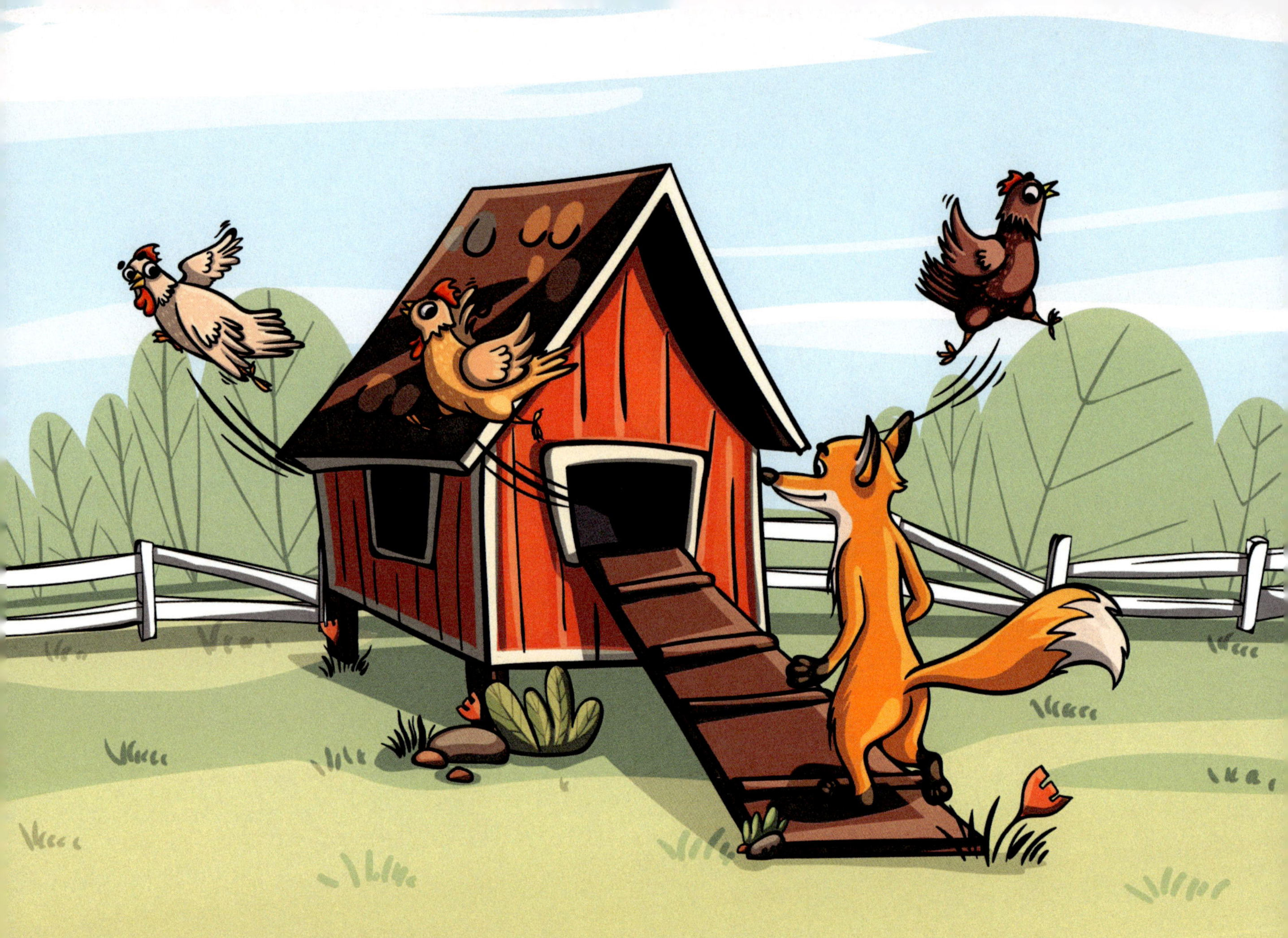

**Peacock needed helpers to share the weight
Getting the ball rolling out of the gate.
The nasty fowl proved that he was a louse
When he put foxes in ev'ry hen house.
He couldn't use rat friends, who were excited,
'Cause most of them ended up indicted.
Why should we be stunned, as hit by a rake?
'Twas no surprise. They were RATS for God's sake!
The bulk of the hires were pigs or pig-sheep.
Soon many of the former fled the creep.**

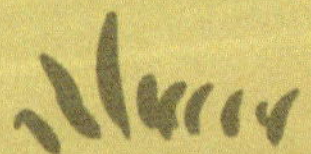

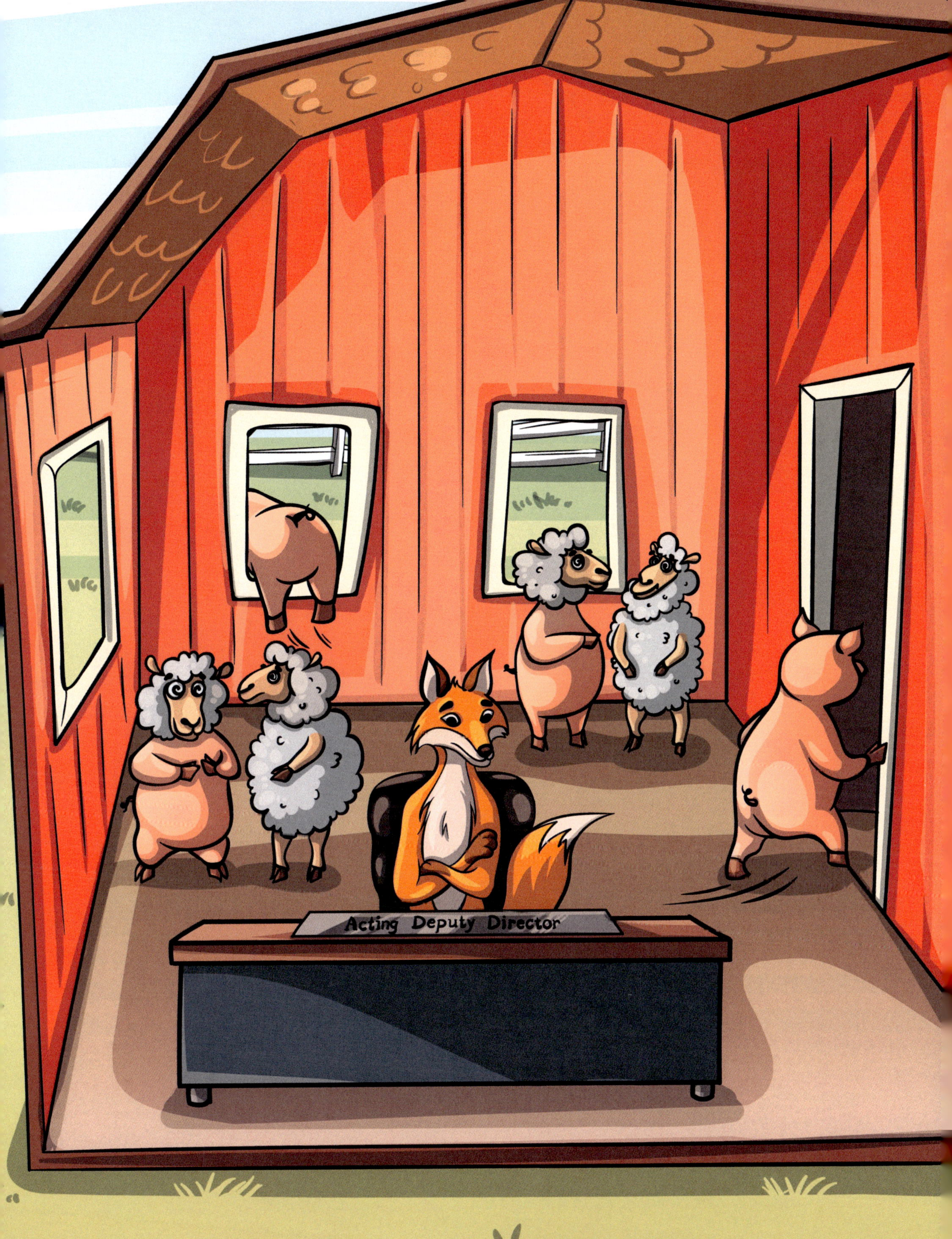
Acting Deputy Director

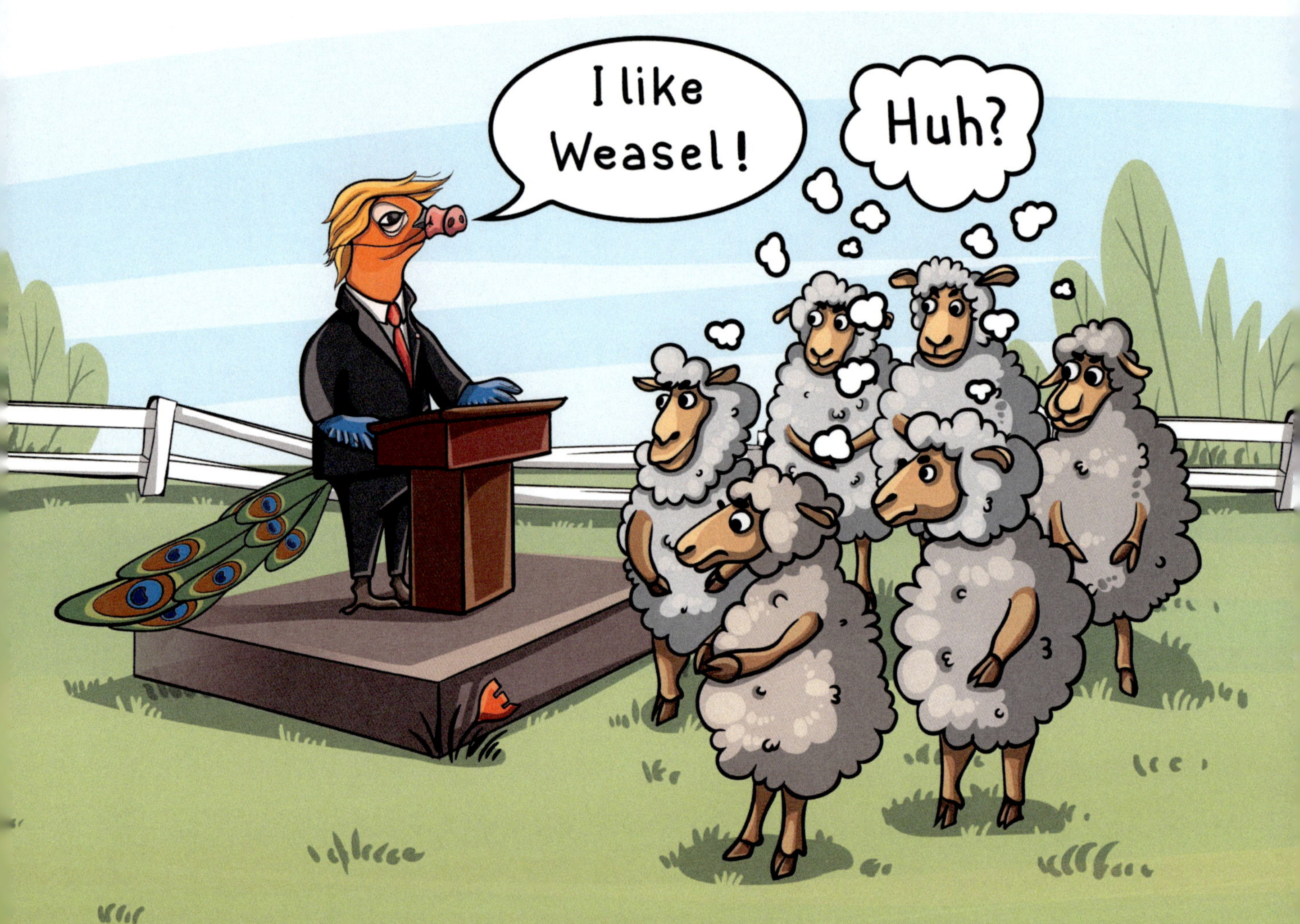

When Peacock continued lie after lie,
It was enough to make honest ones cry.
He made dog-whistle taunts, feathered his nest,
And cozied up to that big weasel pest.
But that peacock still put nary a dent
In his solid base of 40 percent.
Whenever sheep started to be frazzled,
He'd spread his tail and they were redazzled.

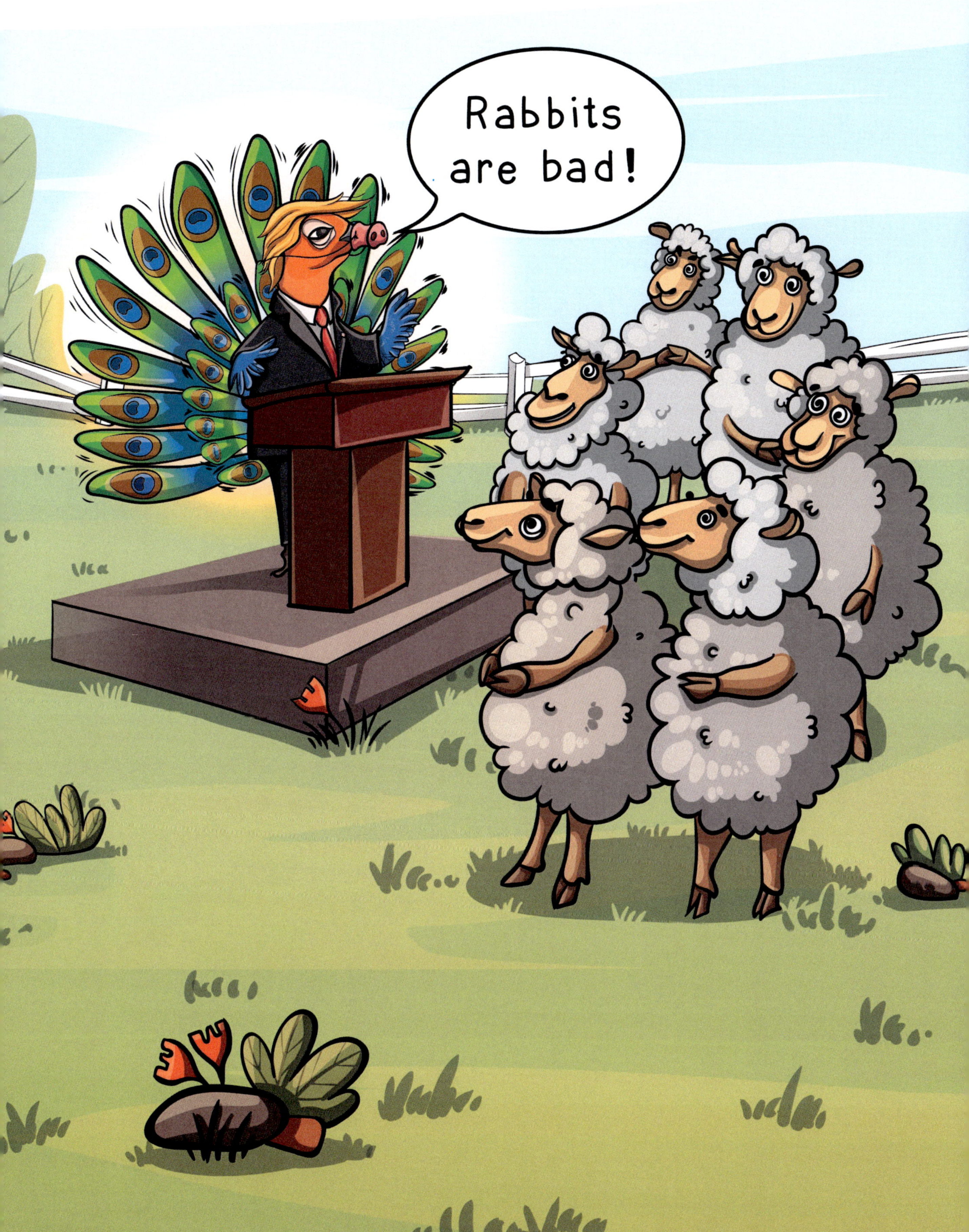
Rabbits
are bad!

What disappointed the horses for sure
Were pigs who had been doctrinally pure
And now were mere sheep with no moral set
Who sat still while Peacock ran up the debt.
The reason was clear, no "if," "and" or "but."
The richest pig-sheep had got their tax cut.

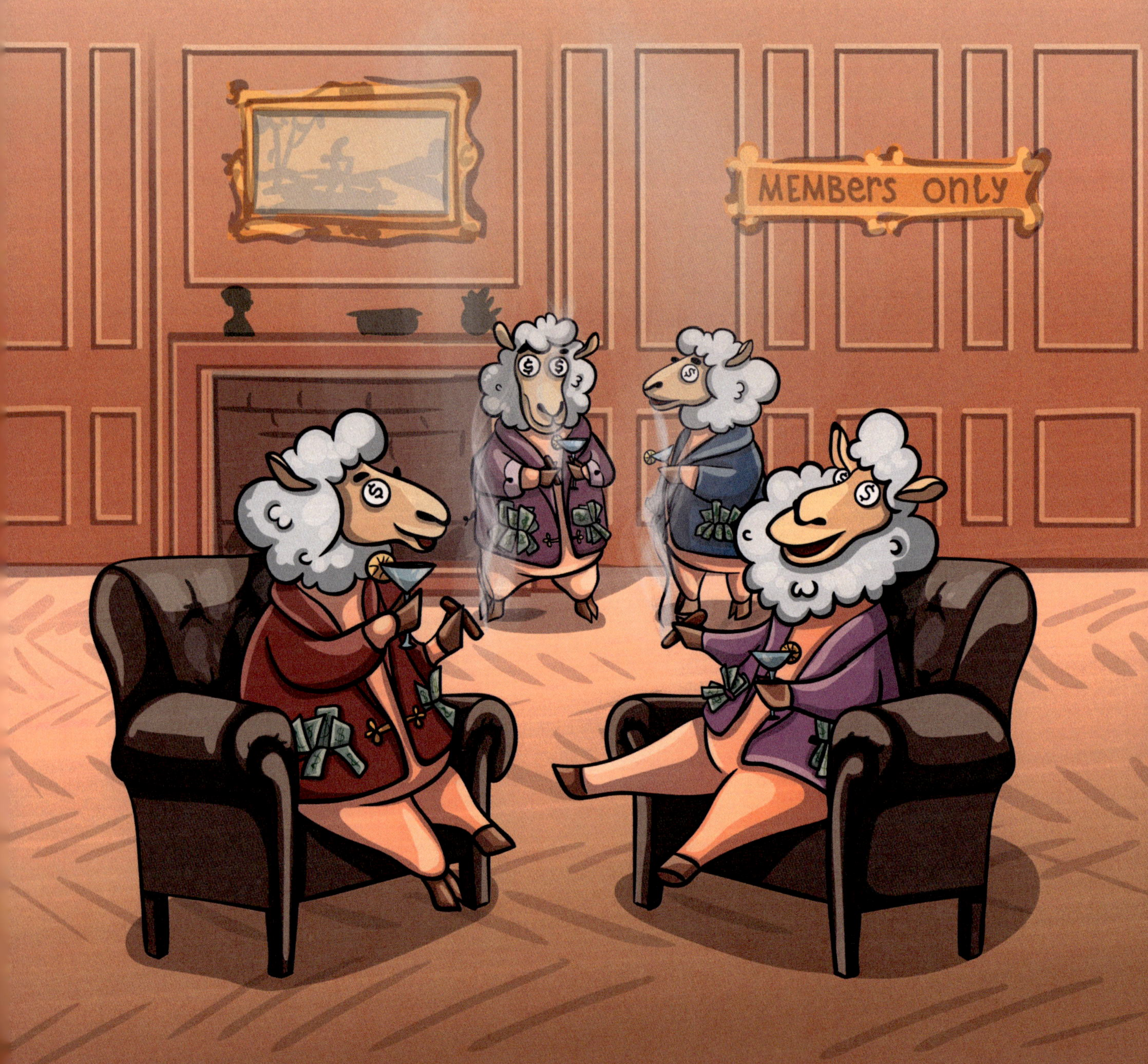

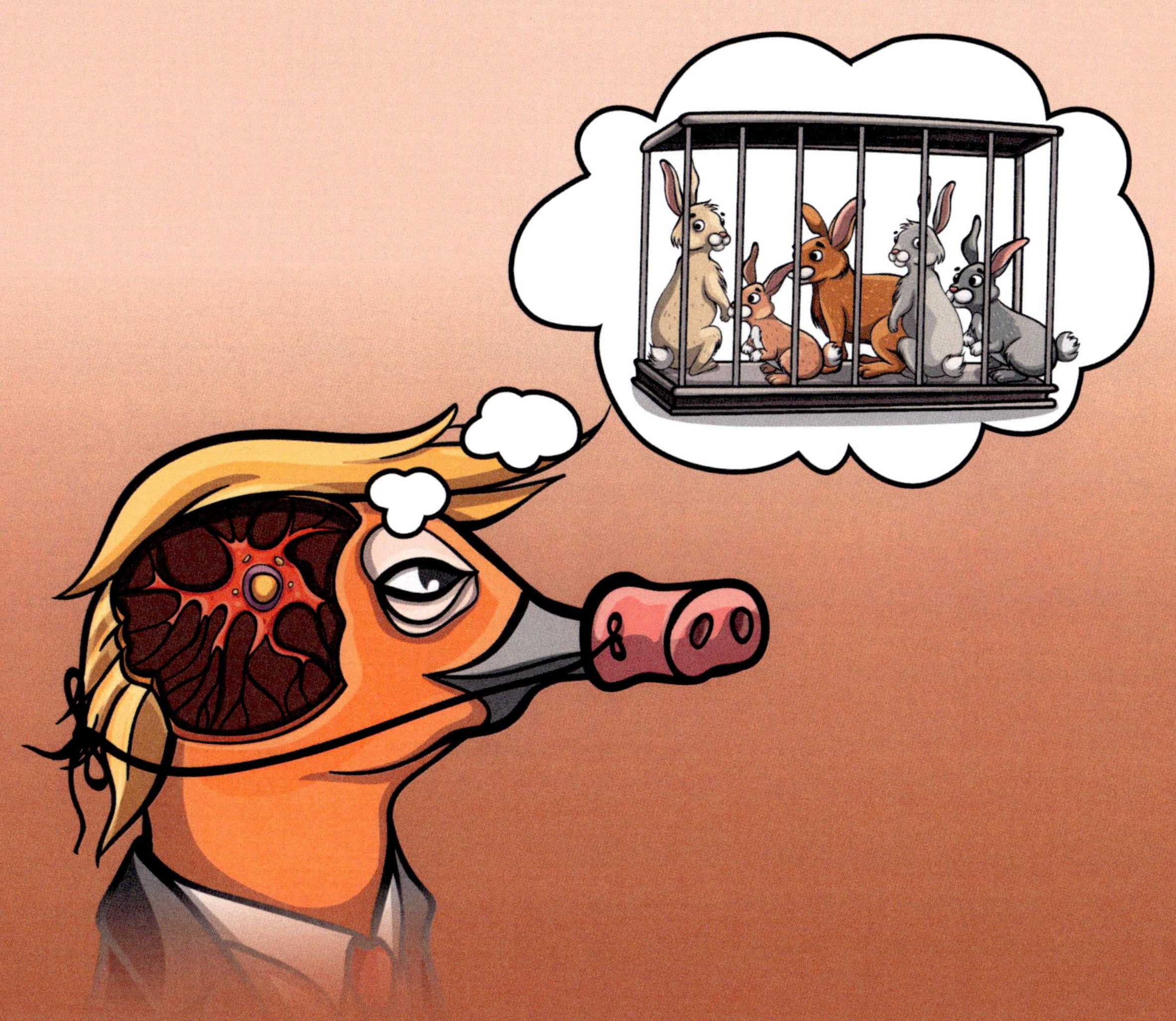

No matter how much bile the peacock spilt,
He just could not get that great big wall built.
His new plan that got his minions humming:
Be mean to the rabbits! They'll stop coming!
Then the peacock did something outrageous.
Took baby bunnies. Put them in cages!
It was a plan, as far as I can tell,
Made by an unaccompanied brain cell.

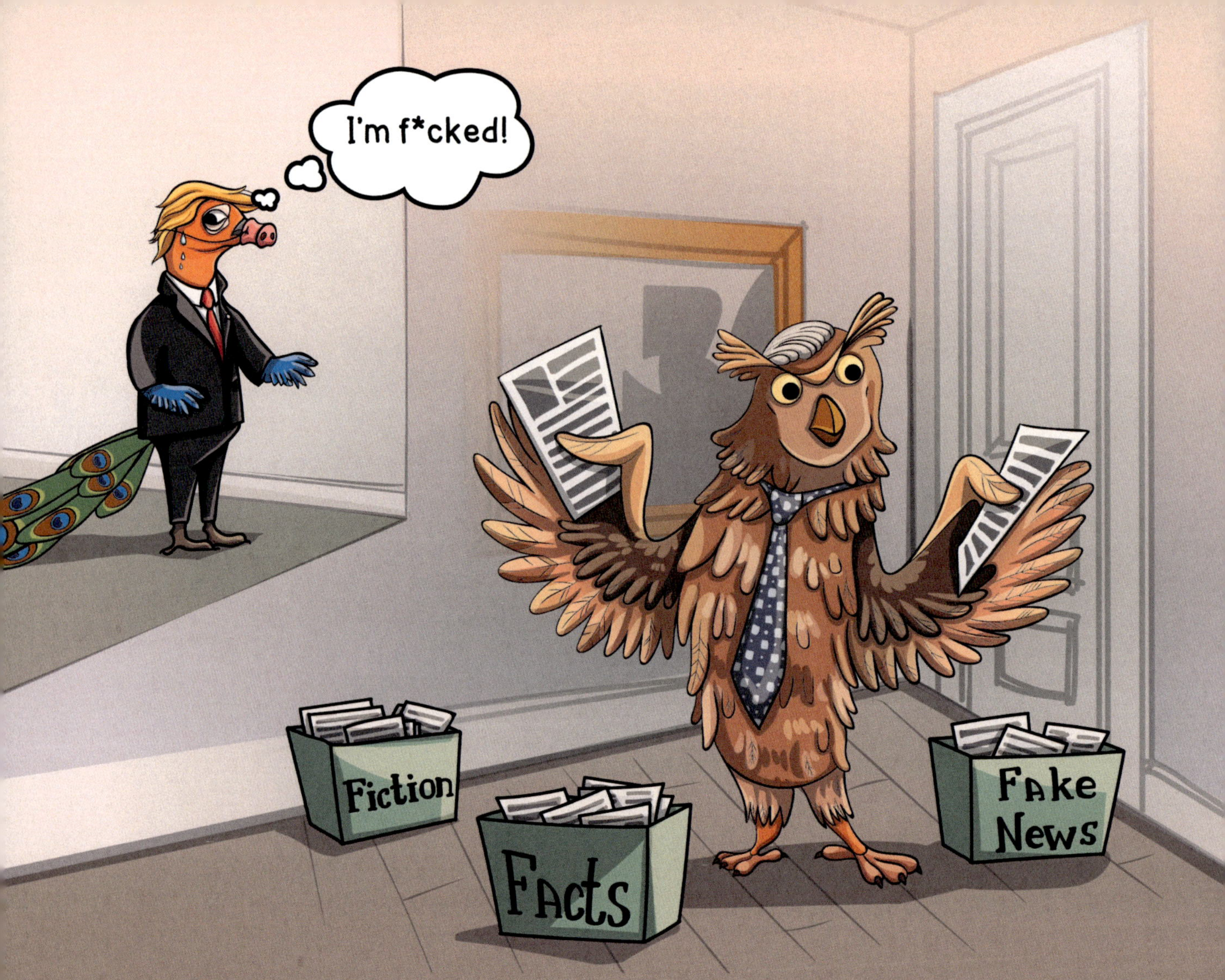

The air was filled with the sound of angry spats
As rumors grew about the peacock's rats:
That they conspired with the weasel despised,
And a weasel's just a rat over-sized.
Someone needed to review campaign acts
To sort out fiction and fake news from facts.
You should've heard the thin-skinned peacock howl
When they gave the job to a wise, old owl.

The owl quietly went about his work
While the peacock pestered him like a jerk.
Finally done, the report took ages.
It went on nearly 500 pages.
Could not prove the campaign had conspired,
Though lots of acts not to be admired.
But Part Two enabled one to deduct
Some 10 ways the peacock tried to obstruct.

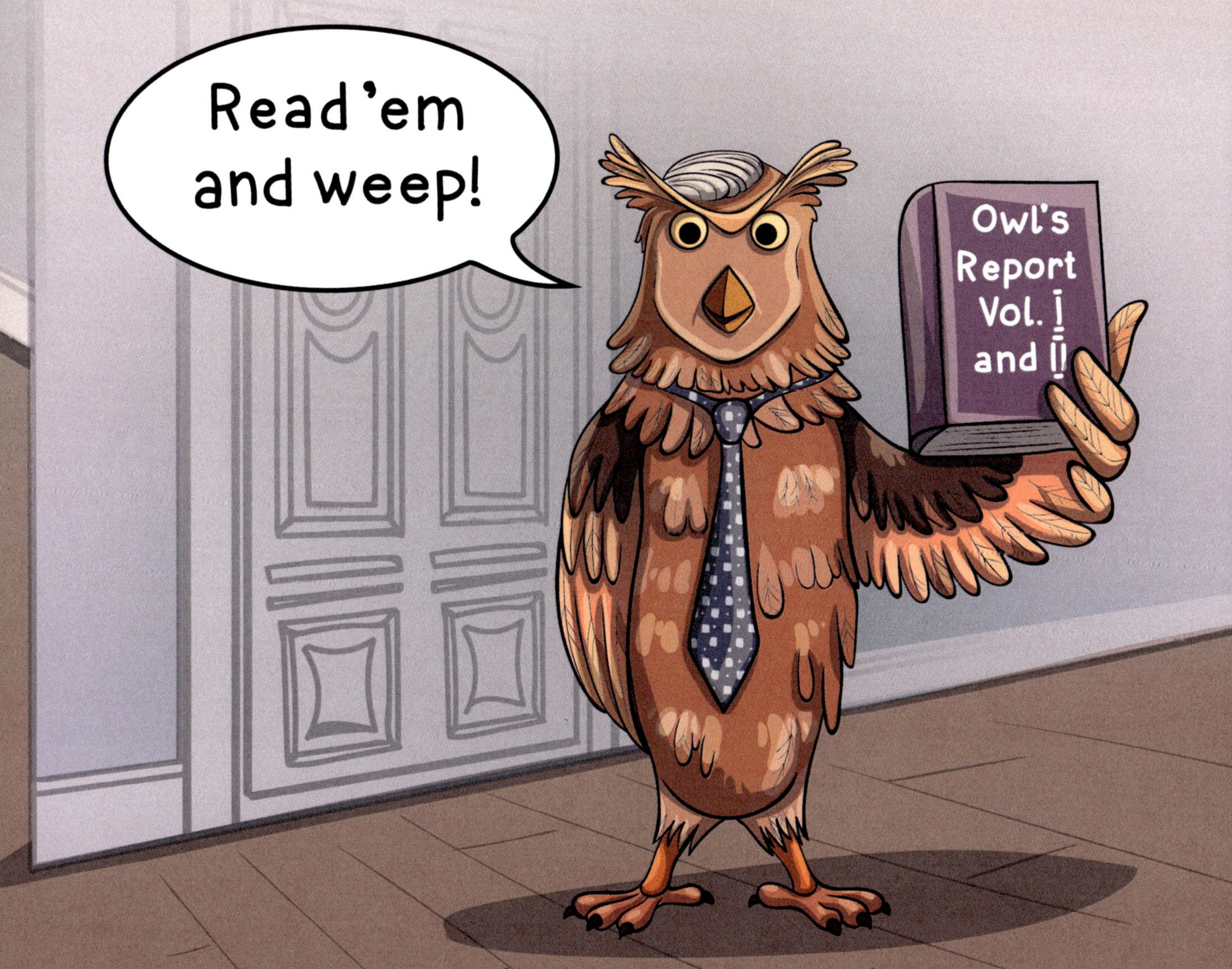

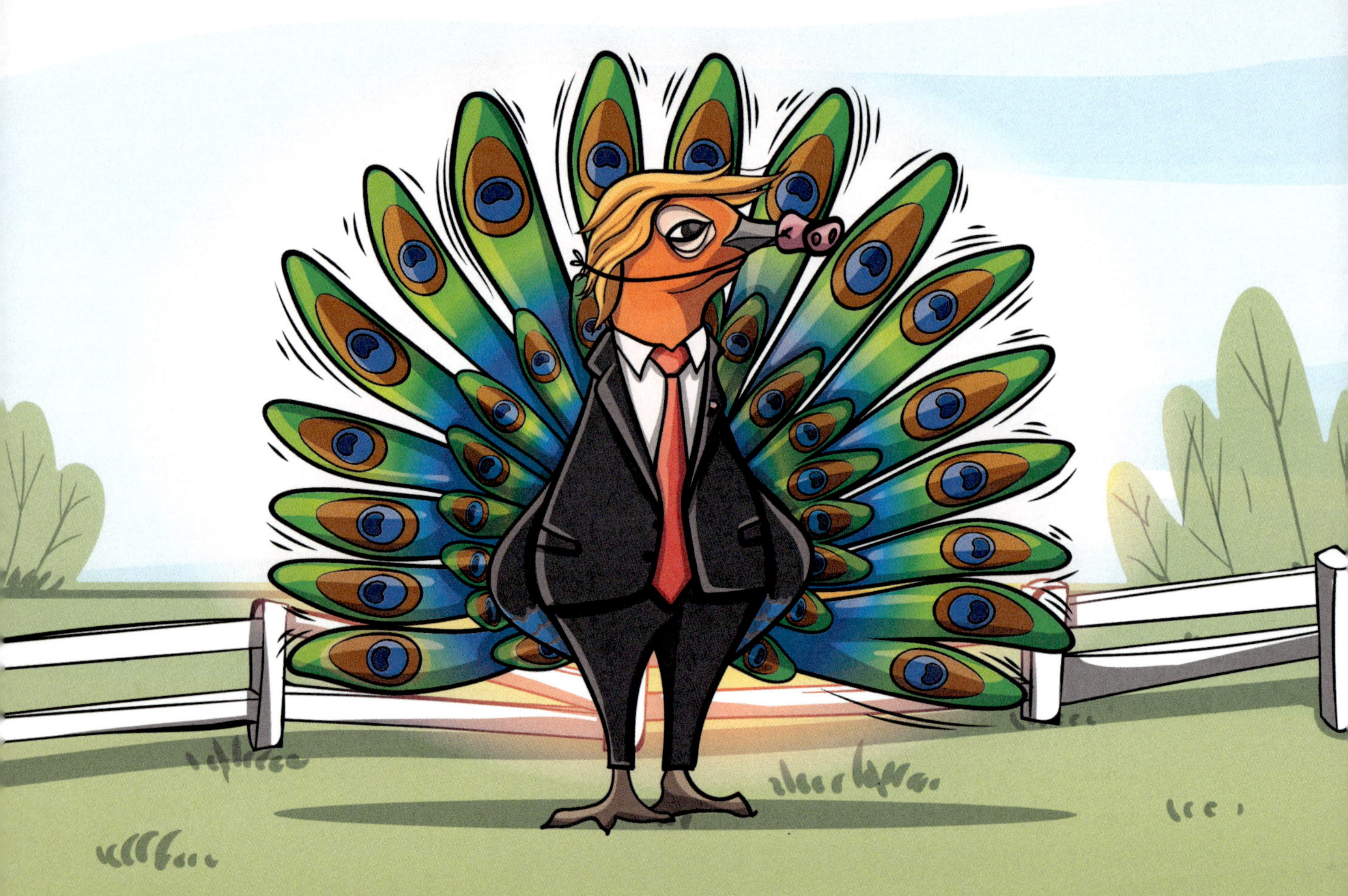

Peacock answered the report with a smirk
And gave his showy tail feathers a twerk.
The public statement by his A.G. toad:
"Nothing to see here. Move on down the road."
The shameless pig-sheep, each one a stinker,
Took the peacock's bait: hook, line and sinker,
Despite a complaint pile from floor to roof.
What if the shoe were on the other hoof?
Would the pig-sheep, self-righteous and pious,
Have afforded a horse the same bias?

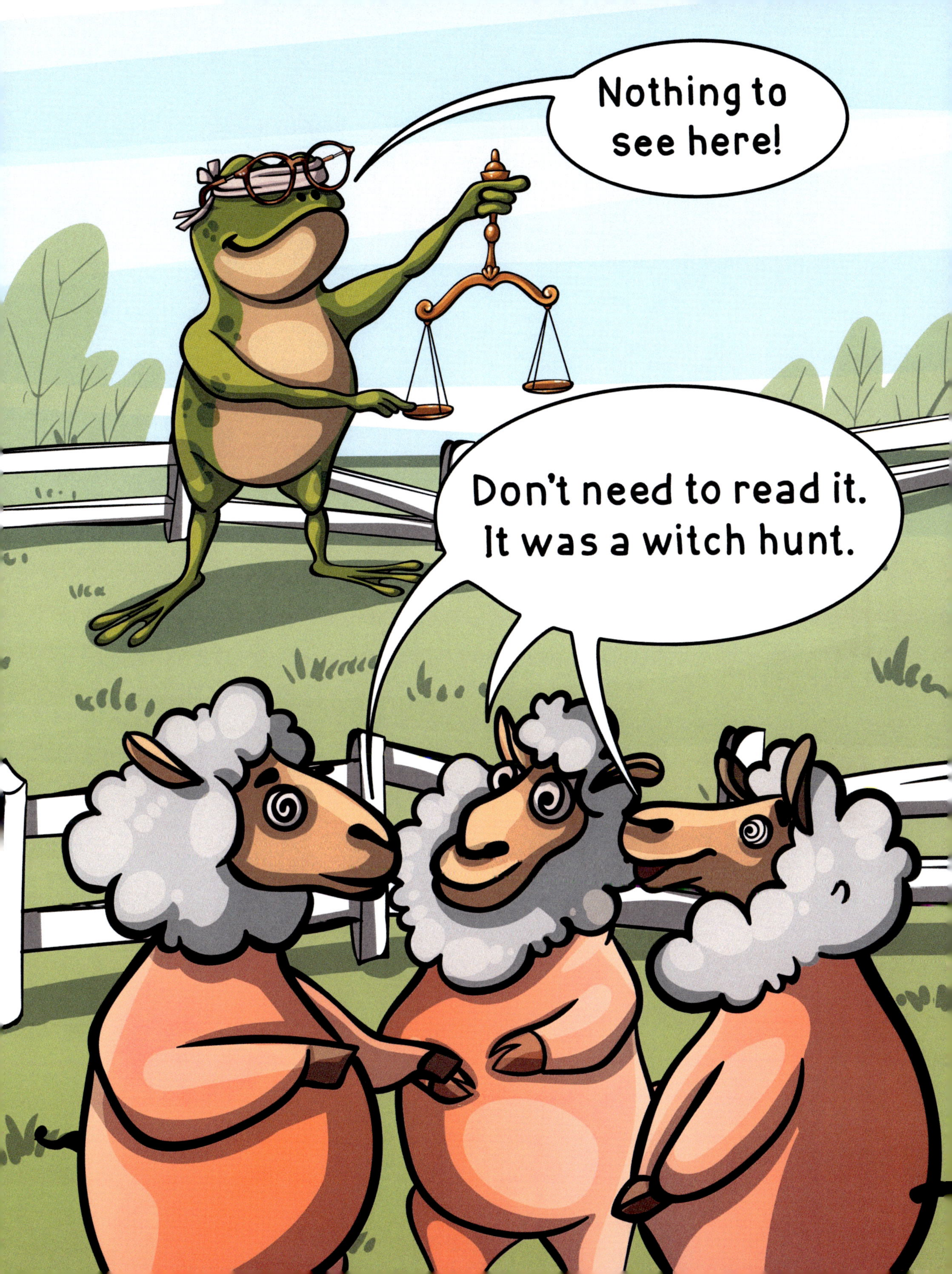
Nothing to see here!
Don't need to read it. It was a witch hunt.

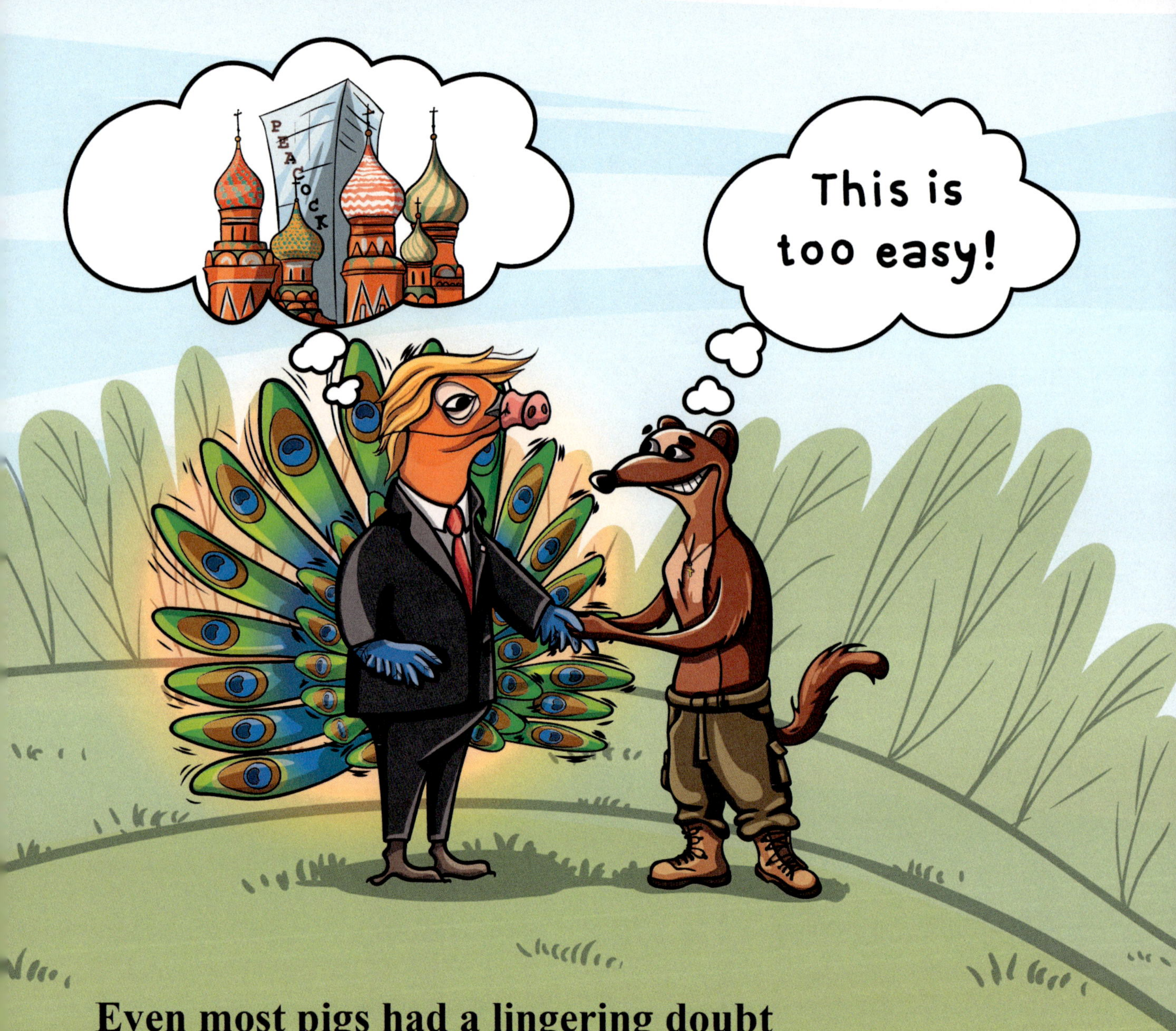

Even most pigs had a lingering doubt
What Peacock and Weasel's ties were about.
Pigs disliked Weasel, more like despised him.
But Peacock never even criticized him.
Many animals had quite bad feelings
About the pair's financial dealings
And the weasel's evil predilection.
What does that mean for the next election?

Soon the animals will get to decide
In what kind of place they want to reside.
Is a leader okay who acts uncouth
And forces on them his version of truth?
Or should they be led by someone who acts
In their best interests based on the facts?
When the animals go into the polls,
All of them should look deep into their souls
As this vote is more important than most.
It may decide if democracy's toast.

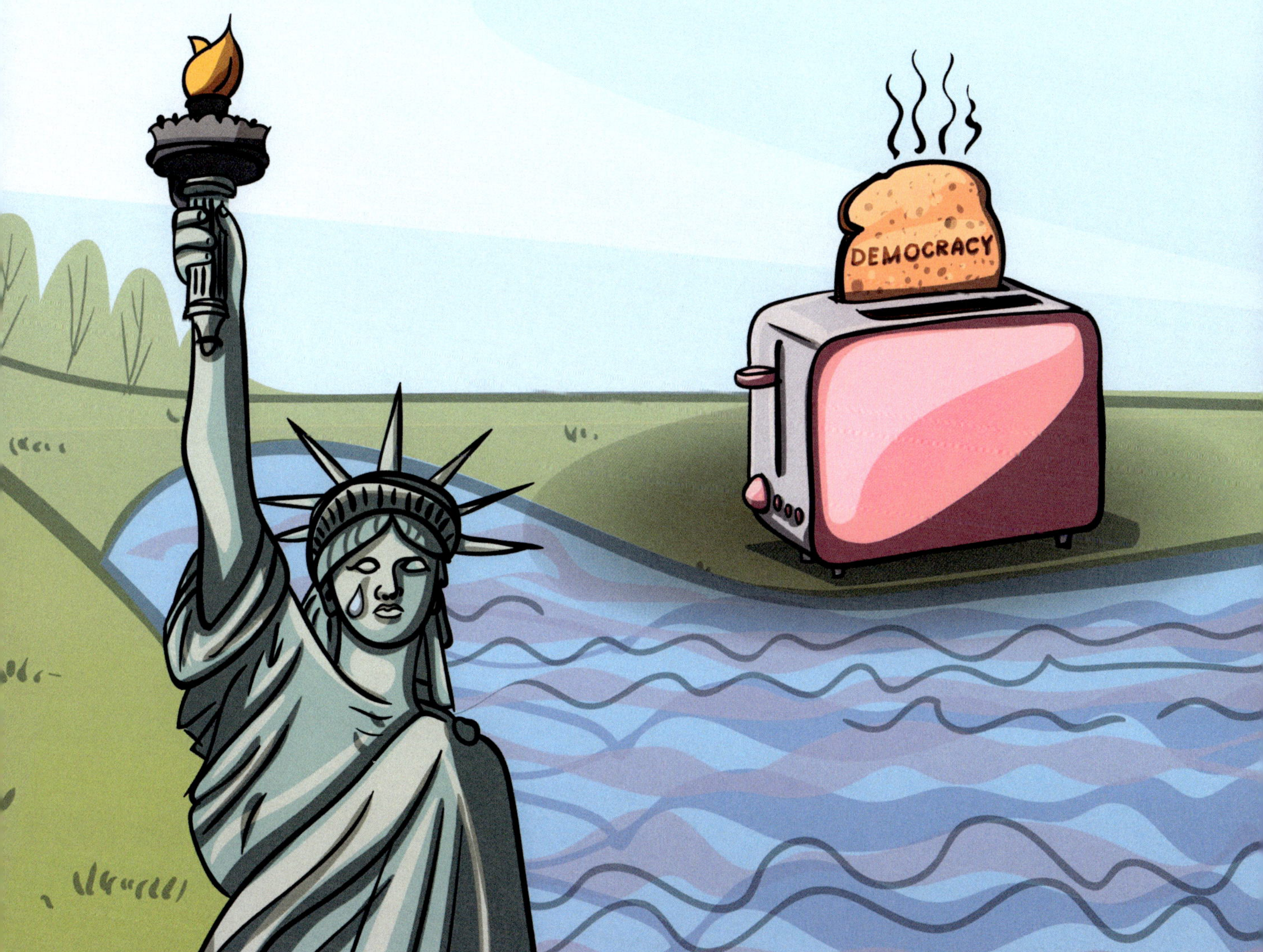

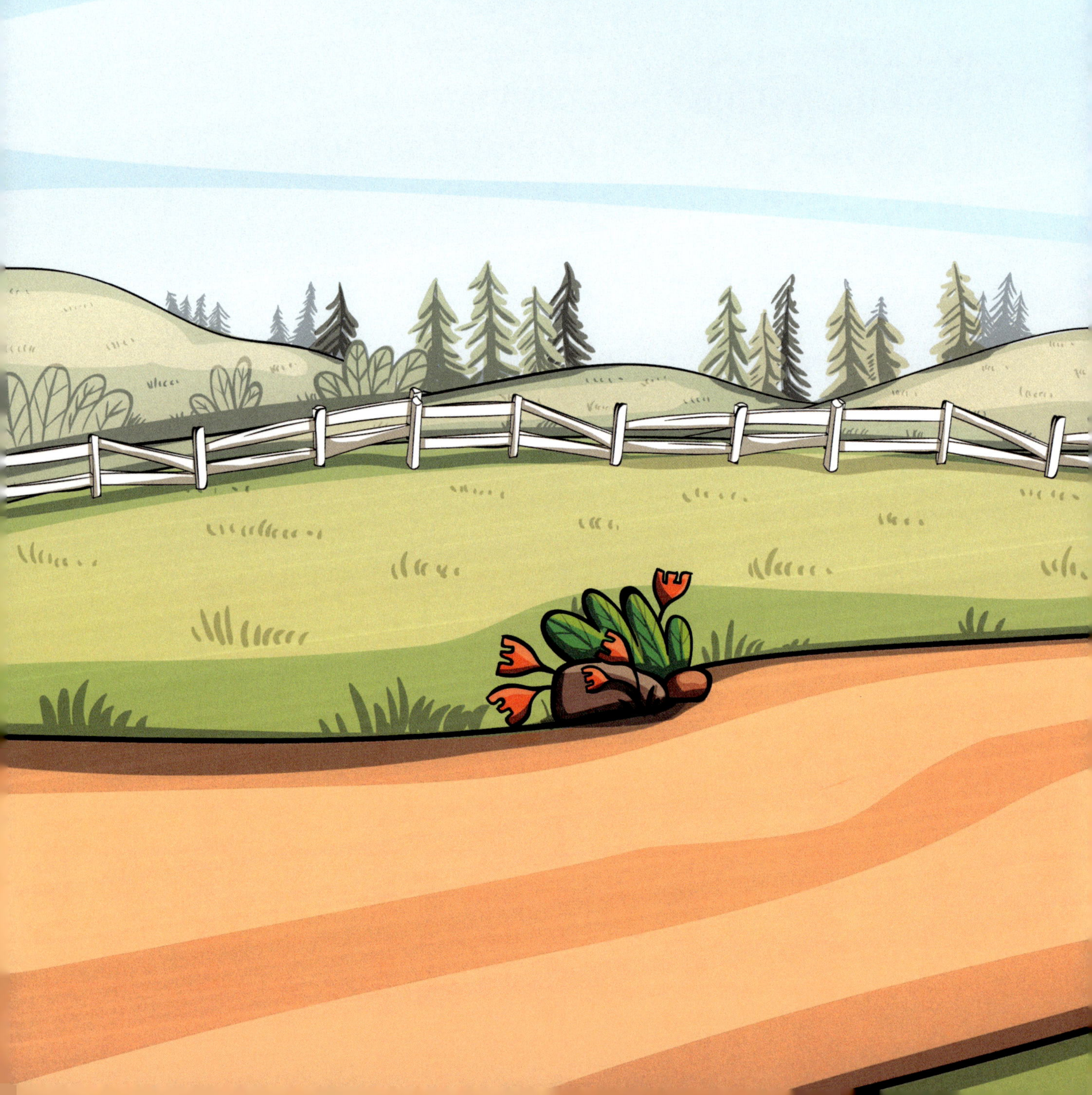

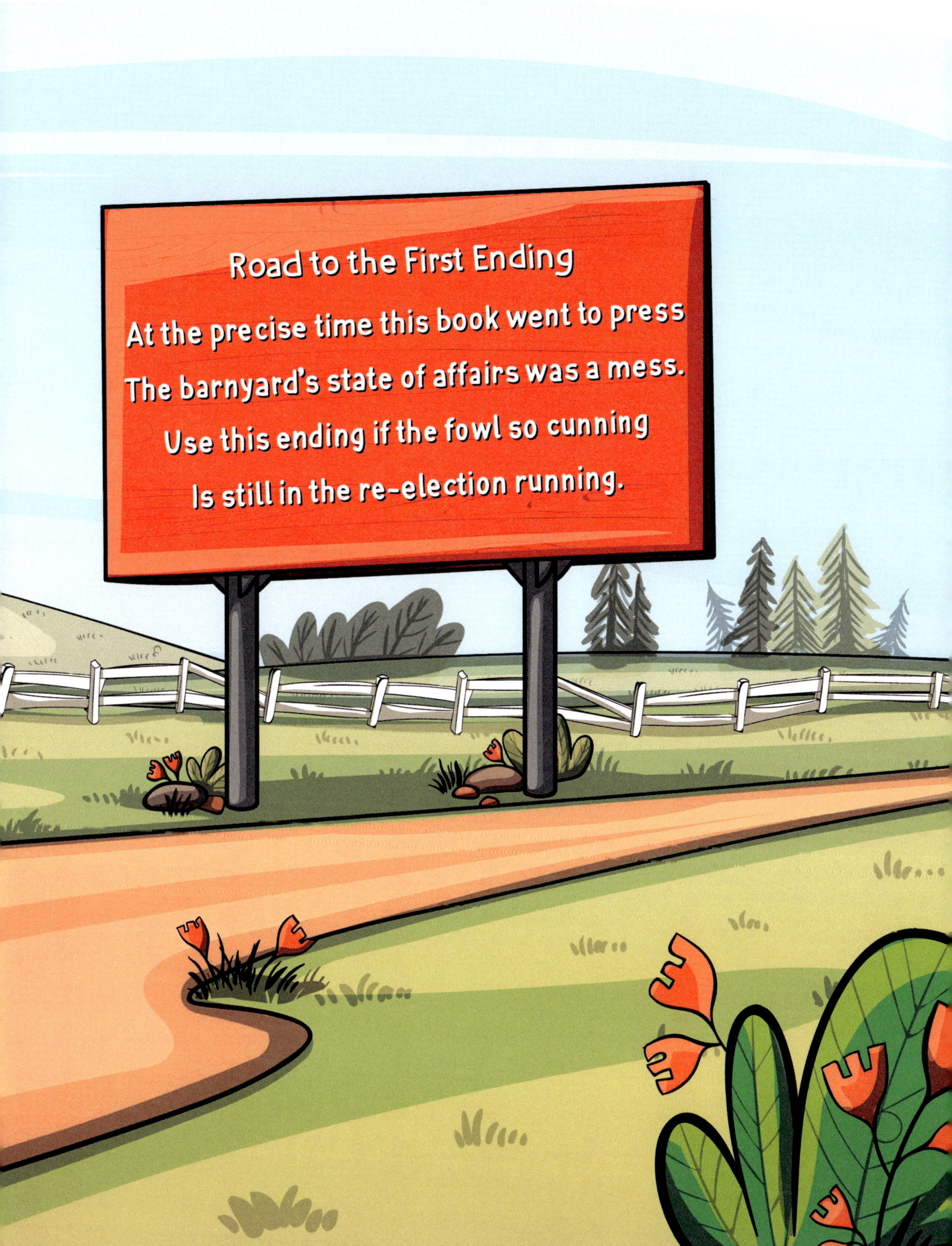
Road to the First Ending
At the precise time this book went to press
The barnyard's state of affairs was a mess.
Use this ending if the fowl so cunning
Is still in the re-election running.

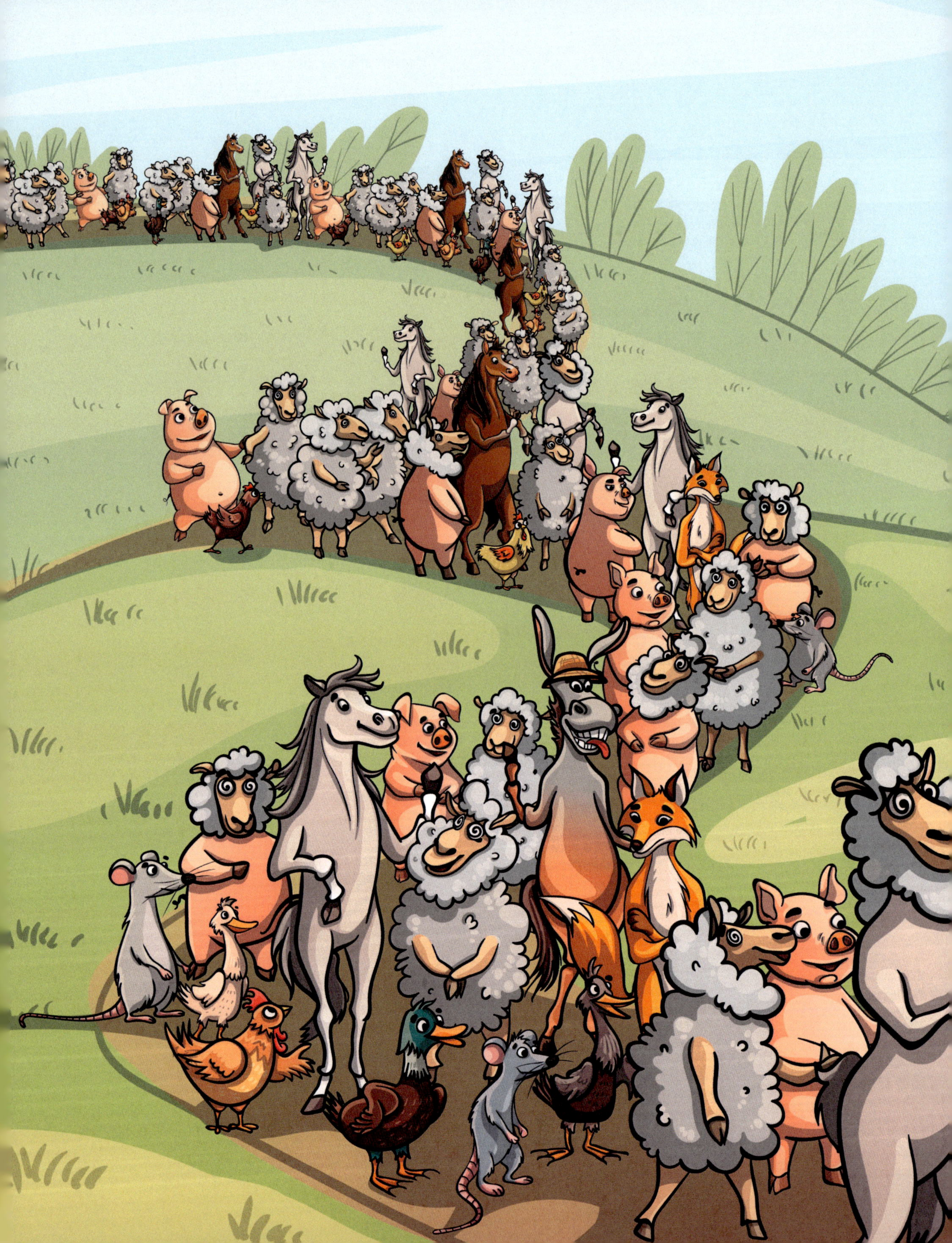

There will be a moral to this story
Of the peacock brimful of vainglory.
When voters return to the polls, you see,
Then we will know what the moral will be.
Will they choose one whose service is for all
Or will it be one obsessed with a wall?
Will they send pig-sheep back to the Senate
When few profiles in courage were in it?
Perhaps the moral IS known, I observe,
The animals will get what they deserve.

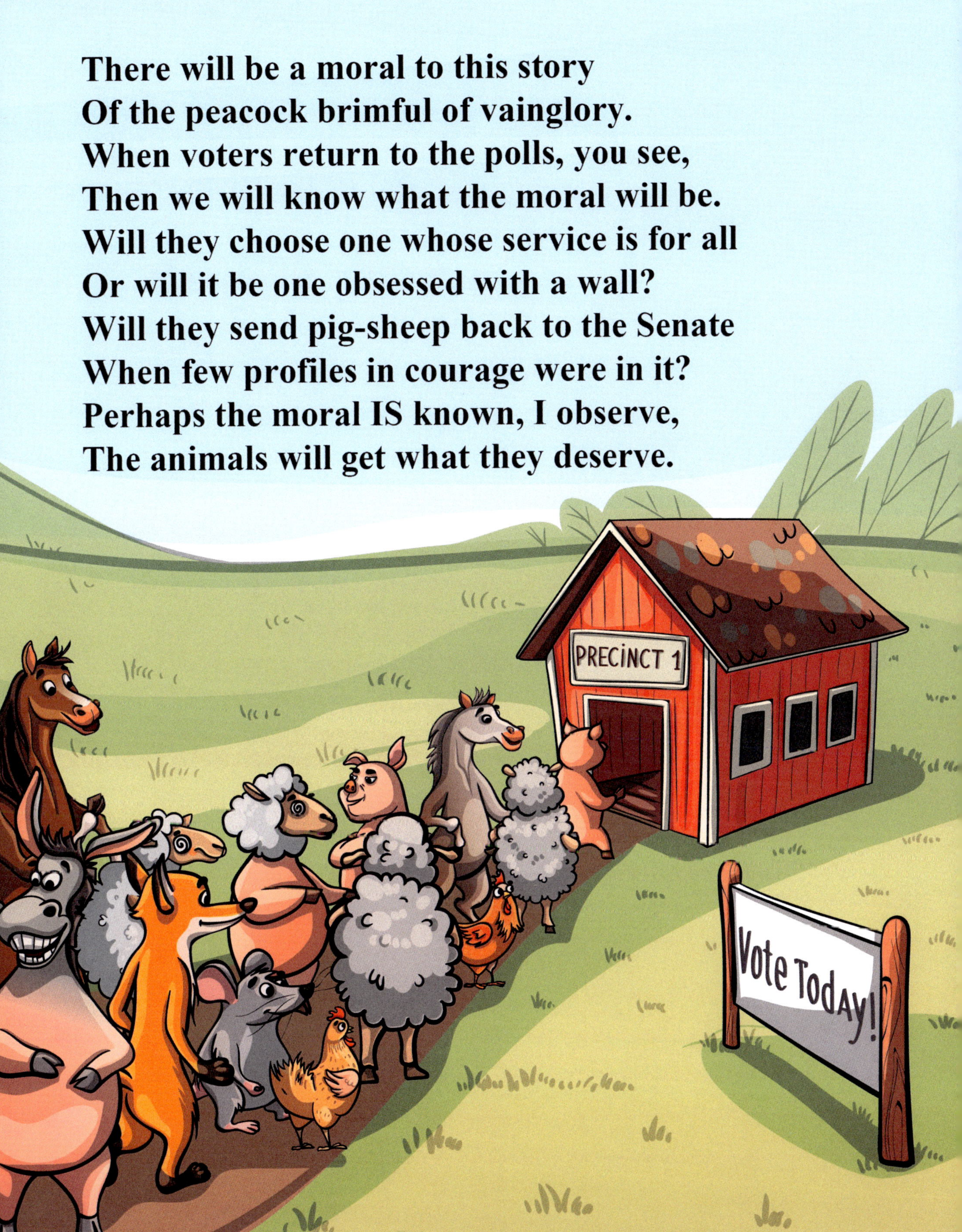

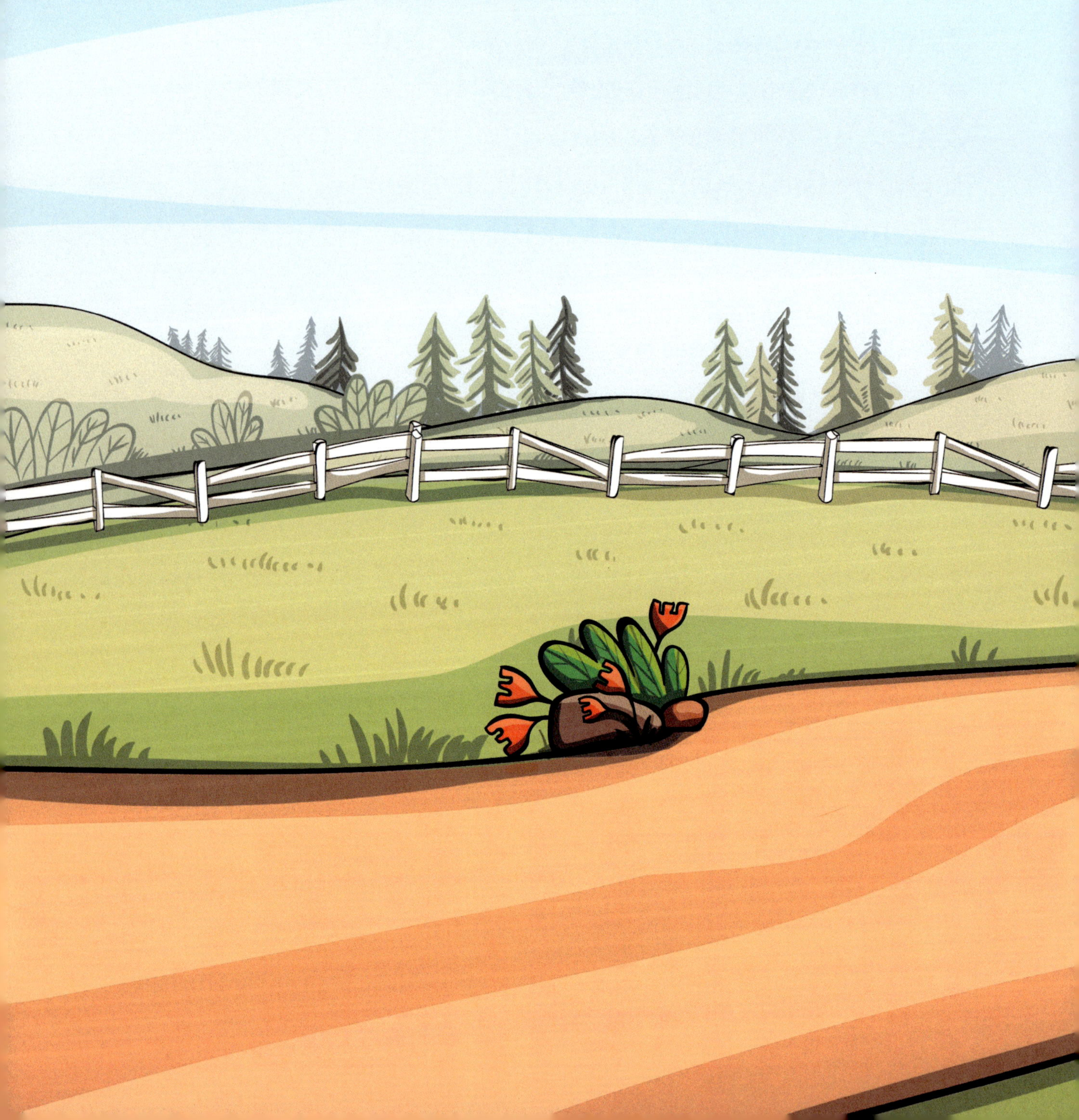

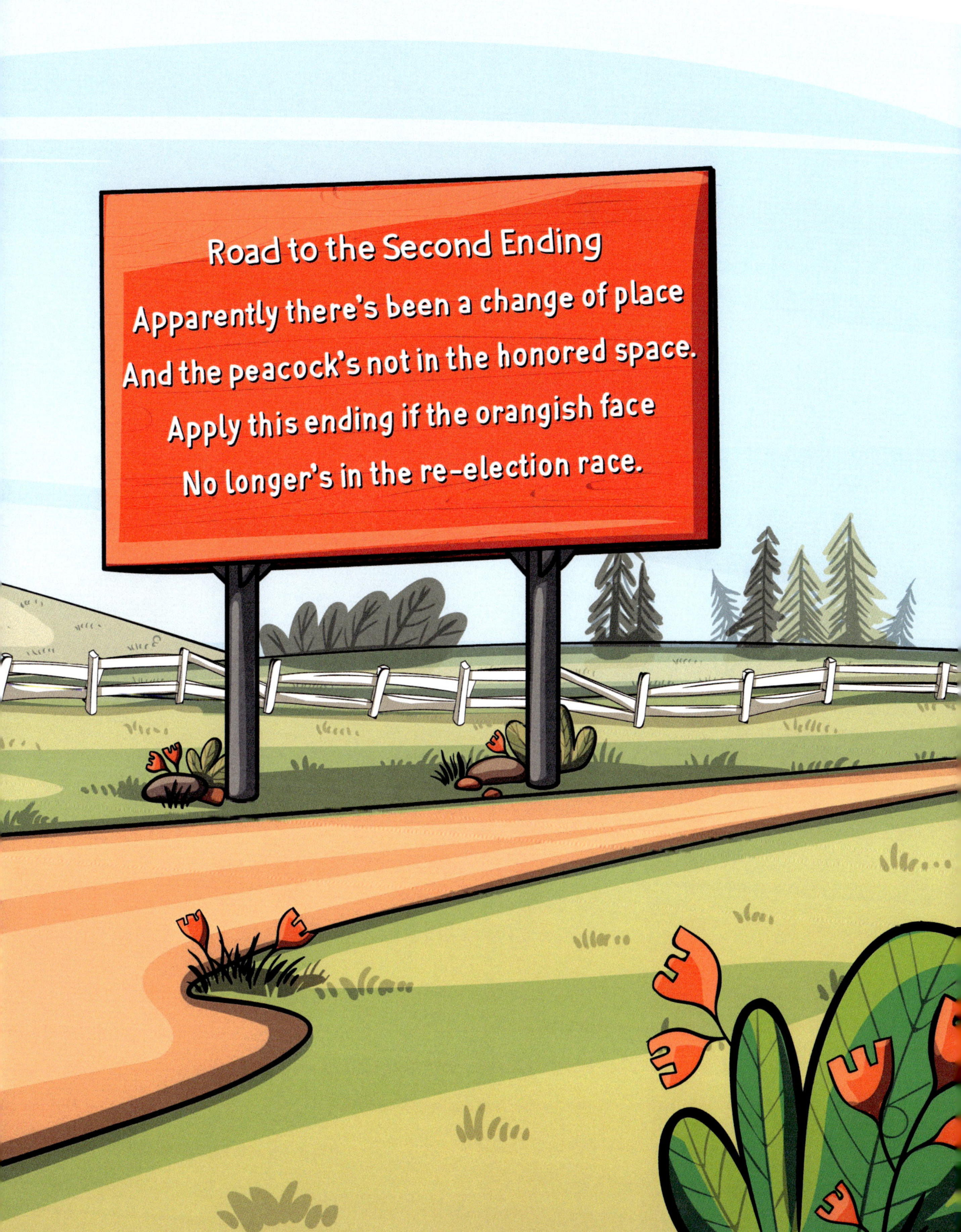
Road to the Second Ending
Apparently there's been a change of place
And the peacock's not in the honored space.
Apply this ending if the orangish face
No longer's in the re-election race.

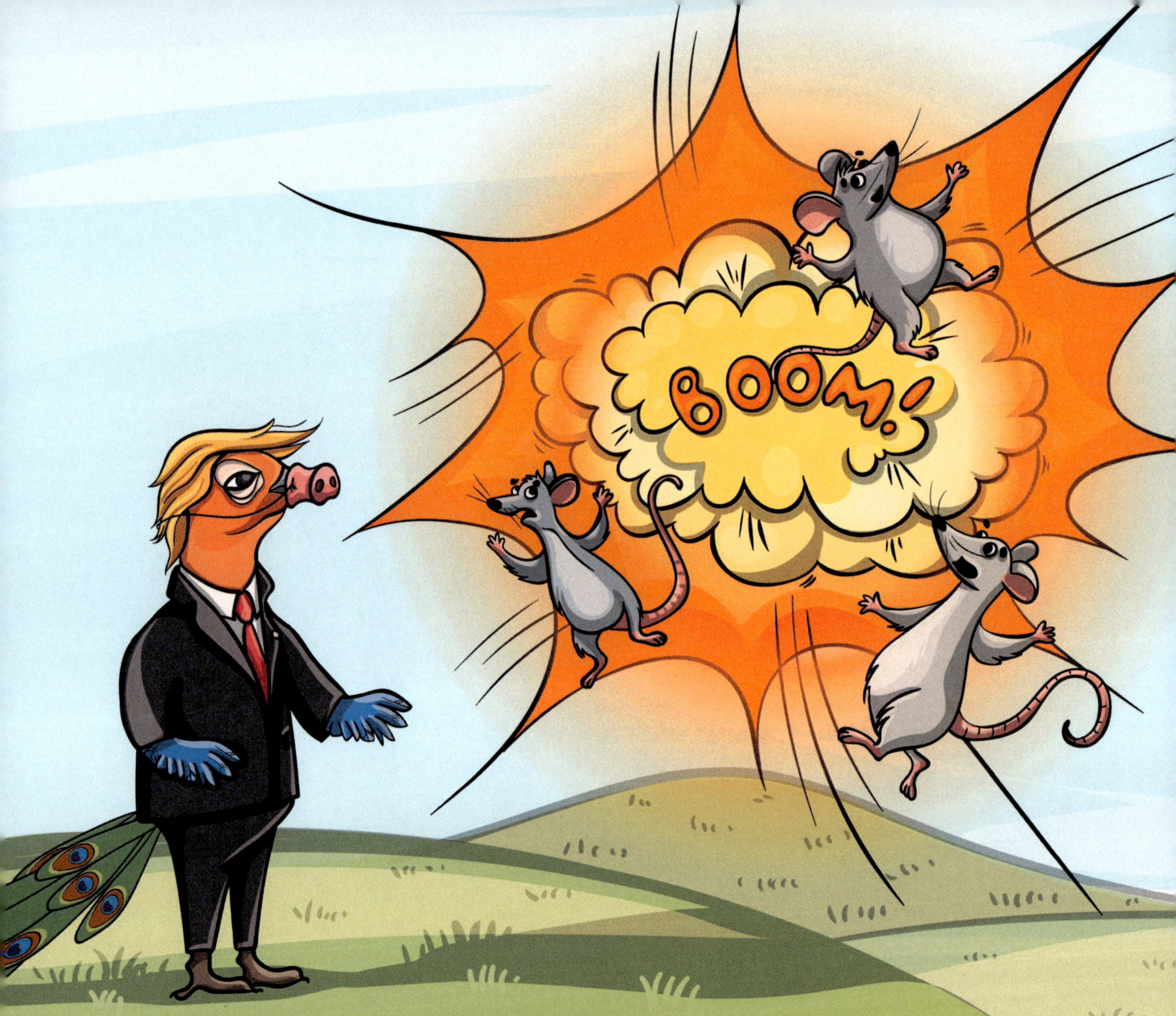

OH! WAIT! What just happened in the barnyard?
Peacock got hoisted with his own petard!
He worked with his rat friends to fix the race
Till his brazen plan blew up in his face.
Always before the enabling pig-sheep
Feared to challenge the misdeeds of the (bleep).
They closed their eyes to all his offenses
Till quid pro quo brought some to their senses.

There are a few lessons in this story
Of the peacock brimful of vainglory.
The first thing we learned from the few years past
Is a beast's true nature will last and last.
Another thing is that when filled with fear
Nature's instinct is to protect one's rear.
Fear of migrant rabbits eating one's grass
Or a primary challenge coming to pass.
What will happen in the next election?
Will the voters make a clear rejection
Of cowardly pig-sheep under fowl's spell
Who put the barnyard through some years of Hell?
The most important moral, I observe,
The animals will get what they deserve.

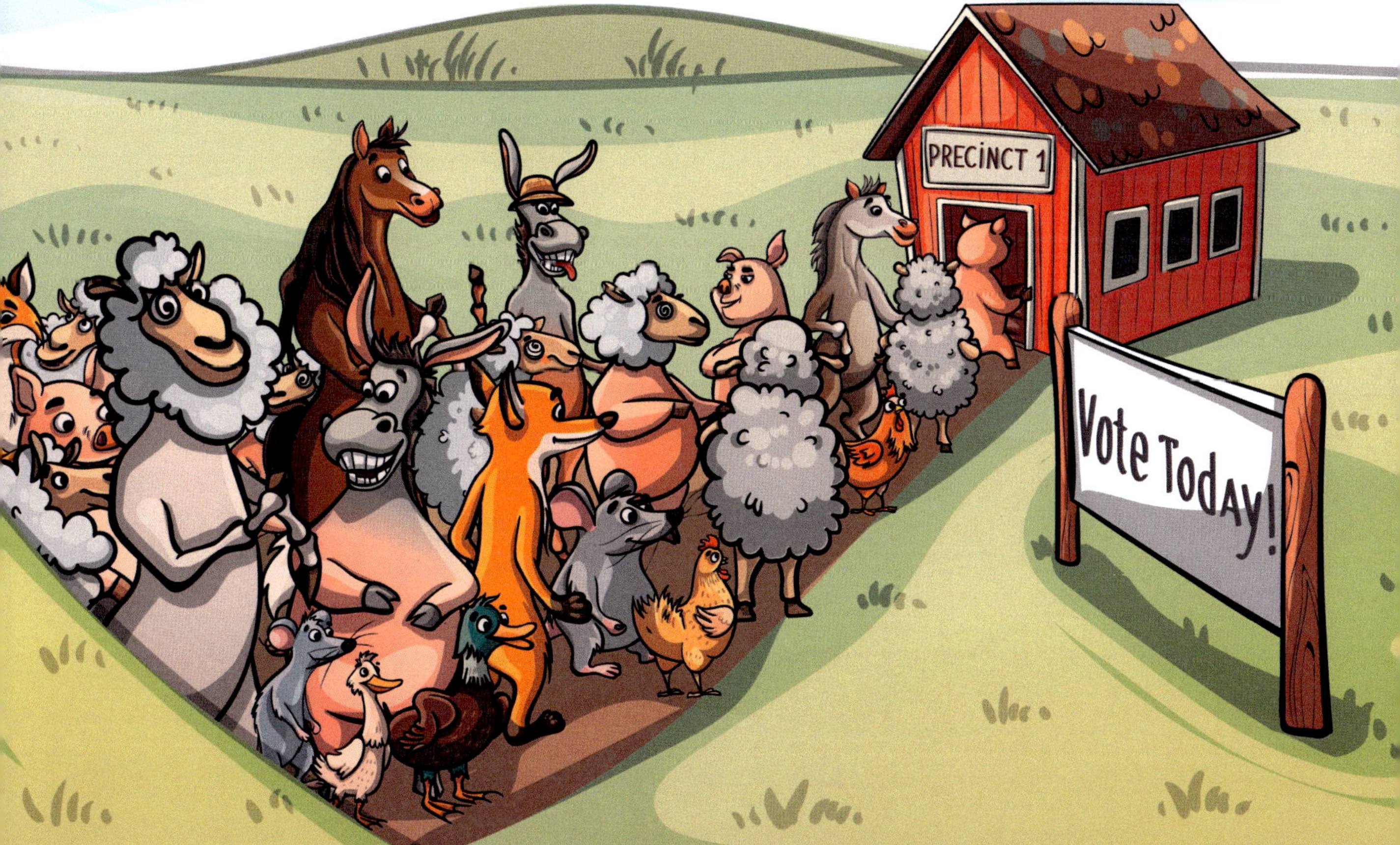

About the Author

Brent Bohlen of Springfield, Illnois, retired from a career in and around state and local government that included being a prosecutor, legal counsel for a taxpayer group and a commissioner on a state public utilities commission. He also authored BoomerWalk, which encourages baby boomers to take up Olympic-style race walking as a highly aerobic, low-impact form of exercise.

About the Illustrator

Oksana Basarab lives and works in Lviv, Ukraine, using Illustrator, Photoshop and sometimes real tools for creativity. She specializes in children's cartoon illustrations. Her portfolio includes more than a dozen books and manuals and countless illustrations for posters, leaflets, patterns, web applications and other products.

About the Publisher

Jeff Salvage of Medford, New Jersey, owner of Salvage America Publications, has published many books under various imprints. He teaches computer science at Drexel University, is an accomplished photographer and was an international athlete.

Website

Please visit *www.peacockparable.com* to shop for merchandise related to ***The Parable of the Peacock*** and to sign up for our email list to stay in touch about future creations.

Made in the USA
Monee, IL
10 November 2019